Super Easy Crock Pot Cookbook for Beginners

1000 Days of Tasty, Effortless, and Foolproof Crock Pot Recipes for Everyday Slow Cooking Meals and Any Occasions

Carey Peterson

Welcome to the "Super Easy Crock Pot Cookbook for Beginners"!
Get ready to embark on a culinary journey filled with delicious and effortless meals. Whether you're new to slow cooking or a seasoned pro looking for simple recipes, this cookbook has you covered.

Inside, you'll find a collection of mouthwatering dishes designed specifically for your crock pot. From hearty stews to savory soups and tender roasts, each recipe is crafted with ease and convenience in mind.

With minimal prep and maximum flavor, cooking has never been simpler. Let's fire up those crock pots and dive into a world of effortless cooking magic
!
Happy cooking!

- **Carey Peterson**

Table of Contents

Introduction

Welcome to the world of slow cooking! If you've ever found yourself longing for delicious, home-cooked meals without the hassle of spending hours in the kitchen, then you're in the right place. The Crock Pot, or slow cooker, is a culinary marvel that has revolutionized the way we approach cooking. In this book, "The Ultimate Crock Pot Cookbook for Beginners," we will embark on a culinary journey together, exploring the ins and outs of slow cooking and discovering an array of mouthwatering recipes that are both simple and satisfying.

Slow cooking isn't just about convenience; it's about elevating the flavors of your favorite dishes to new heights. By allowing ingredients to simmer and meld together over an extended period, the Crock Pot unlocks depths of flavor that traditional cooking methods simply can't match. Whether you're a busy professional, a parent juggling multiple  responsibilities, or simply someone who loves good food without the fuss, the Crock Pot is about to become your new best friend.

In this comprehensive guide, we'll start by laying the groundwork for success in slow cooking. We'll delve into the fundamentals of using a Crock Pot, including essential tips for choosing the right model, understanding cooking times and temperatures, and mastering the art of flavor layering. Even if you're a complete novice in the kitchen, fear not – by the time you've finished reading this book, you'll be wielding your Crock Pot like a seasoned pro.

Next, we'll dive into the heart of the matter: the recipes. From hearty stews and comforting soups to succulent roasts and indulgent desserts, there's something for everyone in these pages. Whether you're craving classic comfort food, exotic flavors from around the world, or healthy, wholesome meals that nourish both body and soul, you'll find plenty of inspiration here. Each recipe is carefully crafted with beginners in mind, with clear instructions, readily available ingredients, and minimal prep work required. So go ahead, dust off that Crock Pot and get ready to embark on a culinary adventure like no other.

But this book is more than just a collection of recipes – it's a celebration of the joys of slow cooking. It's about savoring the process as much as the end result, taking pleasure in the anticipation of a meal that has been lovingly simmering away all day. It's about coming home to the irresistible aroma of a perfectly cooked dish, ready and waiting to be enjoyed. And it's about the simple pleasure of gathering around the table with loved ones, sharing good food and even better company.

As you embark on your slow cooking journey, don't be afraid to get creative. Experiment with different ingredients, flavors, and techniques – after all, that's half the fun! And remember, the beauty of the Crock Pot lies in its versatility. Whether you're cooking for one or feeding a crowd, whether you prefer meat-centric meals or plant-based delights, there's no limit to what you can achieve with a little imagination and a trusty Crock Pot by your side.

So, without further ado, let's roll up our sleeves, fire up those Crock Pots, and get cooking! Whether you're a seasoned chef or a complete beginner, "The Ultimate Crock Pot Cookbook for Beginners" is your ticket to culinary success. Get ready to discover a world of flavor, convenience, and endless possibilities – one delicious recipe at a time. Happy slow cooking!

Getting Started with Your Crock Pot

What is a Crock Pot?

A Crock Pot, also known as a slow cooker, is a versatile kitchen appliance designed to simplify the cooking process by allowing users to prepare meals with minimal effort and oversight. It revolutionized the way many people cook, offering convenience, efficiency, and delicious results.

The Crock Pot consists of a removable stoneware or ceramic pot housed within a heating element. The pot is typically surrounded by an outer casing made of metal or plastic. The design is simple yet effective, providing gentle and consistent heat over an extended period.

The concept of slow cooking dates back centuries, but the modern electric slow cooker was popularized in the 1970s by the Rival Company, which trademarked the name "Crock-Pot." Its invention aimed to address the needs of busy individuals and families who desired home-cooked meals but lacked the time to prepare them.

One of the primary benefits of a Crock Pot is its convenience. Users can simply place ingredients into the pot, set the desired temperature and cooking time, and let the appliance do the rest. This hands-off approach allows individuals to go about their day while the Crock Pot works its magic, slowly simmering and melding flavors together.

Another advantage of using a Crock Pot is its ability to tenderize tough cuts of meat. The low, steady heat breaks down collagen and connective tissues over time, resulting in succulent and flavorful dishes. Whether it's a hearty beef stew, tender pulled pork, or fall-off-the-bone chicken, the

Crock Pot excels at transforming inexpensive cuts of meat into culinary delights.

In addition to meats, the Crock Pot is ideal for preparing soups, stews, chili, casseroles, and even desserts. Its versatility knows no bounds, allowing for a wide range of recipes to be adapted for slow cooking. From breakfast porridge to decadent chocolate lava cake, there's virtually no limit to what can be made in a Crock Pot.

The Crock Pot's energy efficiency is another notable feature. Unlike conventional ovens or stovetops that can consume significant amounts of energy, the slow cooker uses relatively low wattage, making it an economical option for cooking. Additionally, its long cooking times at low temperatures contribute to energy conservation.

Cleanup is also a breeze with a Crock Pot. Most models feature removable stoneware inserts that can be easily cleaned by hand or placed in the dishwasher. This eliminates the hassle of scrubbing pots and pans, further enhancing the appliance's appeal to busy households.

Furthermore, the aroma that fills the home as a meal cooks in the Crock Pot is undeniably inviting. There's something comforting about returning to a house permeated with the scent of a delicious home-cooked meal awaiting consumption.

In recent years, the popularity of Crock Pot cooking has surged, spurred by a growing appreciation for convenience, healthy eating, and budget-friendly meal options. With advancements in technology, modern Crock Pot models offer programmable settings, digital displays, and even Wi-Fi connectivity, allowing users to control and monitor the cooking process remotely via smartphone apps.

Advantages of Cooking with a Crock Pot

Cooking with a crock pot, also known as a slow cooker, offers numerous advantages that make it a popular choice for many households. These advantages stem from its convenience, versatility, and ability to produce flavorful and tender dishes with minimal effort. Here are some key benefits:

1. **Time-saving convenience:** One of the most significant advantages of using a crock pot is its convenience. It allows you to prepare meals with minimal hands-on time. Simply add the ingredients to the pot, set the desired cooking temperature and time, and let it do the work while  you attend to other tasks. This makes it ideal for busy individuals and families.

2. **Tender and flavorful dishes:** The slow cooking process of a crock pot allows flavors to meld together and meats to become incredibly tender. The low, steady heat gently cooks food over several hours, resulting in rich, savory dishes with enhanced flavors and textures.

3. **Versatility:** Crock pots are incredibly versatile appliances that can be used to prepare a wide variety of dishes, including soups, stews, roasts, casseroles, and even desserts. Whether you're cooking a hearty beef stew or a creamy chicken curry, the crock pot can handle it all.

4. **Cost-effective cooking:** Cooking with a crock pot can be cost-effective, as it allows you to use less expensive cuts of meat that become tender and flavorful through the slow cooking process. Additionally, you can make large batches of food at once, which can help save money on groceries and reduce food waste.

5. **Energy efficiency:** Crock pots are relatively energy-efficient appliances compared to traditional ovens or stovetops. They use a fraction of the energy required to heat a conventional oven, making them a more environmentally friendly option for cooking.

6. **Easy cleanup:** Most crock pots feature removable, dishwasher-safe inserts, making cleanup a breeze. After cooking, simply remove the

insert and wash it along with the lid, reducing the time and effort spent on cleaning up after meals.

In conclusion, cooking with a crock pot offers numerous advantages, including time-saving convenience, tender and flavorful dishes, versatility, cost-effectiveness, energy efficiency, and easy cleanup. Whether you're a busy professional, a home cook looking to simplify meal prep, or someone who enjoys delicious, homemade meals with minimal effort, a crock pot can be a valuable addition to your kitchen arsenal.

Tips for Choosing the Right Crock Pot

Choosing the right crock pot can greatly enhance your cooking experience and ensure delicious meals. Here are some tips to help you make the best choice:

1. **Size:** Consider how many people you typically cook for and the quantity of food you usually prepare. Crock pots come in various sizes ranging from small ones ideal for one or two people to large ones suitable for families or gatherings.
2. **Features:** Look for features that match your cooking needs. Some crock pots offer programmable settings, allowing you to set cooking times and temperatures. Others have built-in timers or automatic warming functions to keep your food warm after cooking.
3. **Shape:** Crock pots come in round and oval shapes. Oval-shaped ones are great for cooking whole chickens or large cuts of meat, while round ones are better suited for soups, stews, and chili.
4. **Material:** Choose a crock pot made of durable materials such as ceramic, which distributes heat evenly and retains it well. Avoid pots with non-stick coatings that may wear off over time.
5. **Lid:** A tight-fitting lid is essential for trapping moisture and heat during cooking. Look for a lid with a seal to prevent spills and ensure that flavors are sealed in.
6. **Temperature settings:** Make sure the crock pot you choose has temperature settings that suit your cooking needs. Some models offer low, high, and warm settings, while others have specific temperature ranges for different cooking methods.

7. **Budget:** Set a budget and stick to it. Crock pots come in a wide range of prices, so you're likely to find one that fits your budget while still meeting your needs.
8. **Reviews:** Read reviews from other users to get an idea of the performance and reliability of the crock pot you're considering. Pay attention to feedback on durability, ease of cleaning, and overall satisfaction.

By considering these factors, you can choose a crock pot that suits your cooking style and helps you create delicious meals with ease.

Essential Accessories

Essential accessories vary greatly depending on one's lifestyle, preferences, and needs. However, some items tend to be universally practical and versatile. These accessories enhance daily routines, provide convenience, and even contribute to personal style. Here are some essential accessories that many find indispensable:

- **Wallet:** A compact and organized way to carry cash, cards, and identification. Choose a durable material like leather for longevity.
- **Watch:** Beyond telling time, a watch adds a touch of sophistication to any outfit and keeps you punctual. Opt for a style that suits your taste and lifestyle, whether it's a classic analog or a smartwatch with various functionalities.
- **Bag or Backpack:** Ideal for carrying everyday essentials such as a laptop, water bottle, snacks, and other necessities. Look for a design that balances style and functionality, with comfortable straps and ample compartments.

- **Headphones/Earphones:** Whether for enjoying music, podcasts, or making hands-free calls, quality headphones enhance audio experiences and provide privacy in public spaces.
- **Sunglasses:** Protect your eyes from harmful UV rays while adding a stylish flair to your look. Invest in a pair with UV protection and a design that complements your face shape.
- **Phone Case:** Guard your smartphone against drops, scratches, and other damage with a sturdy case. Choose from a variety of materials and styles to suit your taste and level of protection needed.
- **Keychain:** Keep your keys organized and easy to locate with a keychain or key organizer. Consider options with additional features like a bottle opener or flashlight for added utility.
- **Water Bottle:** Stay hydrated throughout the day by carrying a reusable water bottle. Opt for a durable and leak-proof design that you can refill on the go.
- **Umbrella:** Be prepared for unexpected rain showers with a compact and portable umbrella. Look for one that's sturdy yet lightweight for easy carrying.
- **Portable Charger:** Ensure your devices stay powered up throughout the day with a portable charger or power bank. Choose one with sufficient capacity to recharge your devices multiple times.

These accessories not only serve practical purposes but also reflect personal style and preferences, enhancing both functionality and aesthetics in daily life.

Crock Pot Basics

Understanding Crock Pot Settings

Crock pots, also known as slow cookers, are versatile kitchen appliances designed to simplify meal preparation by cooking food slowly over a long period of time. These devices typically come with various settings, each serving a specific purpose in the cooking process. Understanding these settings is crucial for achieving optimal results and ensuring the safety of your meals.

One common feature found in most crock pots is the temperature control setting. This setting allows users to adjust the cooking temperature according to the type of food being prepared and the desired outcome. The temperature settings usually include options such as low, medium, and high heat.  Low heat is ideal for slow cooking tough cuts of meat or simmering soups and stews over several hours, while medium heat is suitable for faster cooking or keeping dishes warm. High heat can be used for quickly cooking foods or for recipes that require a shorter cooking time.

Another important setting found in many crock pots is the timer function. This feature enables users to program the cooking time, allowing for greater flexibility and convenience. With a timer, you can set your crock pot to start cooking at a specific time and automatically switch to a keep-warm mode once the cooking cycle is complete. This is particularly useful for busy individuals who want to come home to a hot, ready-to-eat meal without having to monitor the cooking process.

Some advanced crock pots may also include additional settings such as programmable cooking modes, which offer preset cooking times and temperatures for specific recipes like chili, roast, or poultry. These pre-programmed settings take the guesswork out of cooking and ensure consistent results every time.

Safety features are also essential to consider when using a crock pot. Many models come equipped with features such as automatic shut-off functions or temperature probes to prevent overheating and ensure that food is cooked to a safe internal temperature. It's important to follow the manufacturer's instructions and safety guidelines when using these appliances to reduce the risk of accidents or foodborne illness.

In conclusion, understanding the settings and features of your crock pot is essential for successful and safe cooking. Whether you're slow-cooking a hearty stew or preparing a quick weeknight meal, knowing how to adjust the temperature, set the timer, and utilize any additional functions will help you make the most of this convenient kitchen appliance. With proper use and care, a crock pot can be a valuable tool for creating delicious, hassle-free meals for you and your family.

Safety Precautions

Crock pots, also known as slow cookers, are incredibly convenient kitchen appliances for preparing delicious meals with minimal effort. However, like any electrical appliance, it's important to follow safety precautions to prevent accidents and ensure safe usage. Here are some essential safety guidelines for using a crock pot:

- **Read the Manual:** Before using your crock pot, carefully read the manufacturer's instructions and safety guidelines. Familiarize yourself with the appliance's features, recommended usage, and any warnings provided.
- **Inspect the Crock Pot:** Before each use, inspect the crock pot for any signs of damage such as cracks, frayed cords, or loose fittings. Do not use a crock pot that appears damaged, as it may pose a safety hazard.
- **Place on a Stable Surface:** Always place the crock pot on a stable, heat-resistant surface, away from the edge of countertops or tables.

Ensure there is sufficient space around the appliance for proper ventilation.

- **Avoid Overfilling:** Follow the manufacturer's recommendations regarding the maximum fill level for your crock pot. Overfilling can lead to spills, uneven cooking, and potential safety hazards. Leave some space at the top for ingredients to expand during cooking.

- **Handle with Care:** The ceramic insert of a crock pot can become very hot during use. Use oven mitts or pot holders when handling the insert or removing the lid to prevent burns.

- **Use the Correct Temperature Setting:** Most crock pots have multiple temperature settings, such as low, high, and sometimes a keep-warm setting. Use the appropriate setting for your recipe and cooking time to ensure food safety and optimal results.

- **Thaw Ingredients Before Cooking:** Do not place frozen ingredients directly into a crock pot, as this can increase the risk of bacterial growth. Thaw meat and other frozen ingredients in the refrigerator before adding them to the crock pot.

- **Monitor Cooking Progress:** While one of the benefits of using a crock pot is the ability to "set it and forget it," it's important to periodically check on your food during the cooking process, especially if you're using a new recipe or cooking on a high setting.

- **Clean Regularly:** After each use, unplug the crock pot and allow it to cool before cleaning. Remove the ceramic insert and wash it with warm, soapy water. Wipe down the exterior of the crock pot with a damp cloth. Never immerse the base of the crock pot in water.

- **Store Safely:** When not in use, store the crock pot in a cool, dry place, away from heat sources and out of reach of children and pets.

By following these safety precautions, you can enjoy delicious meals cooked safely and efficiently in your crock pot.

Cleaning and Maintenance Tips

Cleaning and maintaining your crock pot properly is essential to ensure its longevity and to keep it functioning efficiently. Here are some tips to help you keep your crock pot in top condition:

- **Unplug and Cool Down:** Before cleaning your crock pot, always make sure it is unplugged and has cooled down completely. This prevents any accidents or burns while handling the appliance.
- **Remove Removable Parts:** Most modern crock pots have removable stoneware inserts and lids. Take these parts out carefully and wash them separately.
- **Hand Wash or Dishwasher:** Check the manufacturer's instructions to see if your crock pot parts are dishwasher safe. If they are, you can place them in the dishwasher for easy cleaning. Otherwise, hand wash them using warm, soapy water.
- **Soak Tough Stains:** For stubborn food residues or stains, soak the stoneware insert in warm, soapy water for some time before scrubbing. Avoid using abrasive cleaners or scouring pads as they can damage the surface.
- **Use Baking Soda:** If there are lingering odors in your crock pot, sprinkle baking soda on the stoneware and let it sit for a few hours or overnight. Then, rinse it thoroughly to remove the baking soda and any odors.
- **Clean the Exterior:** Wipe down the exterior of the crock pot with a damp cloth or sponge to remove any spills or stains. Avoid getting water into the electrical components to prevent damage.
- **Dry Thoroughly:** After washing, make sure to dry all parts of the crock pot thoroughly before reassembling or storing it. Moisture left behind can lead to mold growth or rusting.
- **Store Properly:** Store your crock pot in a clean, dry place when not in use. Make sure all parts are completely dry to prevent mold or mildew from developing.
- **Check for Wear and Tear:** Regularly inspect your crock pot for any signs of wear and tear such as cracks, chips, or frayed cords. If you notice any damage, discontinue use and have it repaired or replaced by a qualified professional.
- **Use Liners:** Consider using slow cooker liners to make cleanup even easier. These disposable liners fit inside the stoneware insert and can be discarded after use, minimizing the need for scrubbing.

By following these cleaning and maintenance tips, you can ensure that your crock pot remains in good condition and continues to serve you delicious meals for years to come.

Breakfast Recipes

Shredded Chicken Muffins

Servings: 4
Cooking Time: 2.5 Hours

Ingredients:
- 6 oz chicken fillet, boiled
- 4 eggs, beaten
- 1 teaspoon salt
- 1 teaspoon ground black pepper
- 1 teaspoon olive oil

Directions:
1. With the aid of a fork, shred the chicken fillet, then combine with the eggs, salt, and freshly ground black pepper.
2. The chicken mixture is then placed into the muffin tins after brushing them with olive oil. Place the muffins in the slow cooker.
3. Cook them for 2.5 hours on high with the lid closed.

Nutrition Info:
Per Serving: 155 calories, 17.9g protein, 0.7g carbohydrates, 8.7g fat, 0.1g fiber, 202mg cholesterol, 680mg sodium, 169mg potassium

Broccoli Egg Casserole

Servings: 5
Cooking Time: 3 Hours

Ingredients:
- 4 eggs, beaten
- ½ cup full-fat milk
- 3 tablespoons grass-fed butter, melted
- 1 ½ cup broccoli florets, chopped
- Salt and pepper to taste

Directions:
1. In a mixing bowl, whisk the milk and eggs.
2. Melted butter should be used to grease the CrockPot's bottom.
   Place the broccoli florets and egg mixture in the crockpot.
3. To taste, add salt and pepper to the food.
   Cook for 2 hours on high or 3 hours on low while covering the pan.

Nutrition Info: Calories per serving: 217; Carbohydrates:4.6 g; Protein: 11.6g; Fat: 16.5g; Sugar: 0.7g; Sodium: 674mg; Fiber: 2.3g

Bacon Eggs

Servings: 2
Cooking Time: 2 Hours

Ingredients:
- 2 bacon

slices

- 2 eggs, hard-boiled, peeled
- ¼ teaspoon ground black pepper
- 1 teaspoon olive oil
- ½ teaspoon dried thyme

Directions:

1. Add some dried thyme and freshly ground black pepper to the bacon.
2. The eggs will then be wrapped in bacon and dusted with olive oil.
   Cook the eggs in the crock pot for two hours on high.

Nutrition Info: Per Serving: 187 calories, 12.6g protein, 0.9g carbohydrates, 14.7g fat, 0.2g fiber, 185mg cholesterol, 501mg sodium, 172mg potassium.

Squash Butter

Servings: 4
Cooking Time: 2 Hours
Ingredients:

- 1 cup butternut squash puree
- 1 teaspoon allspices
- 4 tablespoons applesauce
- 2 tablespoons butter
- 1 teaspoon cornflour

Directions:

1. All ingredients should be combined thoroughly in the crock pot.

2. After that, secure the lid and cook the butter for two hours on high.
3. Put the well-cooled cooked squash butter in the plastic container.

Nutrition Info: Per Serving: 78 calories, 0.2g protein, 6.3g carbohydrates, 5.8g fat, 0.8g fiber, 15mg cholesterol, 44mg sodium, 20mg potassium

Bacon Potatoes

Servings: 4
Cooking Time:
5 Hours
Ingredients:

- 4 russet potatoes
- 1 teaspoon dried thyme
- 4 teaspoons olive oil
- 4 bacon slices

Directions:

1. Olive oil and dried thyme are sprinkled over the cut potatoes.
   After that, split each piece of bacon in half.
2. Place the bacon slices on top of the potatoes in the Crock Pot bowl.
3. Cook them for five hours on high with the lid shut.

Nutrition Info: Per Serving: 290 calories, 10.6g protein, 33.9g carbohydrates, 12.8g fat, 5.2g fiber, 21mg cholesterol, 452mg sodium, 976mg potassium.

Coconut Oatmeal

Servings: 6
Cooking Time: 5 Hours

Ingredients:
- 2 cups oatmeal
- 2 cups of coconut milk
- 1 cup of water
- 2 tablespoons coconut shred
- 1 tablespoon maple syrup

Directions:
1. Carefully combine all the ingredients in the crock pot. After that, cover the pot and simmer the oatmeal for 5 hours.

Nutrition Info: Per Serving: 313 calories, 5.4g protein, 25.8g carbohydrates, 22.5g fat, 4.8g fiber, 0mg cholesterol, 16mg sodium, 316mg potassium

Basil Sausages

Servings: 5
Cooking Time: 4 Hours

Ingredients:
- 1-pound Italian sausages, chopped
- 1 teaspoon dried basil
- 1 tablespoon olive oil
- 1 teaspoon ground coriander
- ¼ cup of water

Directions:
1. Before placing the chopped sausages in the crock pot, season them with ground coriander and dried basil.
2. Add water and olive oil. Sausages should be cooked for 4 hours on high with the lid closed.

Nutrition Info: Per Serving: 338 calories, 12.9g protein, 0.6g carbohydrates, 31.2g fat, 0g fiber, 69mg cholesterol, 664mg sodium, 231mg potassium.

Caramel Pecan Sticky Buns

Servings: 4
Cooking Time: 2 Hours 40 Minutes

Ingredients:
- ¾ cup packed brown sugar
- 15 ounces refrigerated biscuits
- 1 teaspoon ground cinnamon
- 6 tablespoons melted butter
- ¼ cup pecans, finely chopped

Directions:

1. In a bowl, combine brown sugar, cinnamon, and chopped nuts.
   Refrigerator biscuits are coated with melted butter and then dipped in a brown sugar mixture.
2. Layer the biscuits in the crock pot after greasing it.
3. Add the last of the brown sugar mixture on top, then secure the lid.
4. Before serving, cook for about two hours on HIGH.

Nutrition Info: Calories: 583 Fat: 23.5g Carbohydrates: 86.2g

Chorizo Eggs

Servings: 4
Cooking Time: 1.5 Hours
Ingredients:

- 5 oz chorizo, sliced
- 4 eggs, beaten
- 2 oz Parmesan, grated
- 1 teaspoon butter, softened

Directions:

1. Butter the bottom of the crock pot.
   Cook them for 30 minutes on high after adding the chorizo. After that, flip the chorizo slices and add the eggs and Parmesan.

2. Cook the meal for an additional hour on high with the lid closed.

Nutrition Info: Per Serving: 278 calories, 18.6g protein, 1.5g carbohydrates, 21.9g fat, 0g fiber, 208mg cholesterol, 638mg sodium, 200mg potassium

Broccoli Omelet

Servings: 4
Cooking Time: 2 Hours
Ingredients:

- 5 eggs, beaten
- 1 tablespoon cream cheese
- 3 oz broccoli, chopped
- 1 tomato, chopped
- 1 teaspoon avocado oil

Directions:

1. Place the mixture of eggs and cream cheese in the slow cooker.
   Add tomato, broccoli, and avocado oil.
2. Cook the omelet on high for two hours with the lid shut.

Nutrition Info: Per Serving: 99 calories, 7.9g protein, 2.6g carbohydrates, 6.6g fat, 0.8g fiber, 207mg cholesterol, 92mg sodium, 184mg potassium.

Orange Pudding

Servings: 4
Cooking Time: 4 Hours
Ingredients:
- 1 cup carrot, grated
- 2 cups of milk
- 1 tablespoon cornstarch
- 1 teaspoon vanilla extract
- ½ teaspoon ground nutmeg

Directions:
1. Place the carrots in the slow cooker.
2. Add milk, vanilla bean paste, and nutmeg powder.
3. Cornstarch is then added, and the mixture is stirred until it dissolves.
4. For four hours, cook the pudding on low.

Nutrition Info: Per Serving: 84 calories, 4.3g protein, 10.8g carbohydrates, 2.6g fat, 0.8g fiber, 10mg cholesterol, 77mg sodium, 161mg potassium.

Egg Scramble

Servings: 4
Cooking Time: 2.5 Hours
Ingredients:
- 4 eggs, beaten
- 1 tablespoon butter, melted
- 2 oz Cheddar cheese, shredded
- ¼ teaspoon cayenne pepper
- 1 teaspoon ground paprika

Directions:
1. Combine eggs, cheese, cayenne pepper, and ground paprika in a bowl.
2. After that, add the mixture to the crock pot and cover it.
3. For two hours, cook it on high.
4. Scramble the eggs after removing the lid.
5. Cook the meal for 30 minutes on high with the lid closed.

Nutrition Info: Per Serving: 147 calories, 9.2g protein, 0.9g carbohydrates, 12g fat, 0.2g fiber, 186mg cholesterol, 170mg sodium, 88mg potassium.

Eggs with Brussel Sprouts

Servings: 4
Cooking Time: 6 Hours
Ingredients:
- 1 cup Brussel sprouts, halved
- ½ cup Mozzarella, shredded
- 5 eggs, beaten
- 1 teaspoon chili powder
- 1 teaspoon olive oil

Directions:
1. Fill the crock pot with olive oil. The Brussels sprout layer should then be added.
2. Add eggs and chili powder to the vegetables.

3. After that, top with mozzarella and cover.
4. For six hours, cook the food on low.

Nutrition Info: Per Serving: 110 calories, 8.8g protein, 2.9g carbohydrates, 7.5g fat, 1.1g fiber, 206mg cholesterol, 110mg sodium, 172mg potassium

Apricot Oatmeal

Servings: 4
Cooking Time: 4 Hours
Ingredients:
- 1 ½ cup oatmeal
- 1 cup of water
- 3 cups of milk
- 1 cup apricots, pitted, sliced
- 1 teaspoon butter

Directions:
1. Oatmeal is placed in the crock pot.
2. Add the milk, butter, and water.
   Cook the mixture for an hour on high with the lid shut.
3. After that, carefully stir in the apricots and cover the pot with the oatmeal.
   For three hours, cook the food on low.

Nutrition Info: Per Serving: 235 calories, 10.5g protein, 34g carbohydrates, 7g fat, 3.9g fiber, 18mg cholesterol, 97mg sodium, 317mg potassium

Raspberry Chia Pudding

Servings: 2
Cooking Time: 2 Hours
Ingredients:

- 4 tablespoons chia seeds
- 1 cup of coconut milk
- 2 teaspoons raspberries

Directions:
1. Chia seeds and coconut milk should be combined in a crock pot and cooked for two hours on low heat.
2. Add raspberries on top of the cooked chia pudding after it has been placed in the glasses.

Nutrition Info: Per Serving: 423 calories, 7.7g protein, 19.6g carbohydrates, 37.9g fat, 13.1g fiber, 0mg cholesterol, 23mg sodium, 442mg potassium.

Creamy Bacon Millet

Servings: 6
Cooking Time: 4 Hrs 10 Minutes
Ingredients:
- 3 cup millet
- 6 cup chicken stock
- 1 tsp salt

- 4 tbsp heavy cream
- 5 oz. bacon, chopped

Directions:
1. Fill the crock pot with chicken stock and millet.
2. Season with salt and the chopped bacon.
3. Put the lid on the cooker and select a High cooking setting for 4 hours.
4. Add the cream and once again secure the Crock Pot's lid.
5. On high, cook for 10 minutes.
6. Serve.

Nutrition Info: Per Serving: Calories 572, Total Fat 17.8g, Fiber 9g, Total Carbs 83.09g, Protein 20g

Chia Oatmeal

Servings: 2
Cooking Time: 8 Hours
Ingredients:
- 2 cups almond milk
- 1 cup steel cut oats
- 2 tablespoons butter, soft
- ½ teaspoon almond extract
- 2 tablespoons chia seeds

Directions:
1. Mix the oats, chia seeds, and other ingredients in your Crock Pot; toss; cover; and cook on low for 8 hours.

2. The oatmeal is stirred one more time, then divided into two bowls and served.

Nutrition Info: calories 812, fat 71.4, fiber 9.4, carbs 41.1, protein 11

Carrot Pudding

Servings: 4
Cooking Time: 5 Hours
Ingredients:
- 3 cups carrot, shredded
- 1 tablespoon potato starch
- 3 tablespoons maple syrup
- 1 teaspoon ground cinnamon
- 4 cups of milk

Directions:
1. Pour the mixture of milk and potato starch into the crock pot.
   Add carrots, maple syrup, and ground cinnamon.
2. Put the lid on and cook the pudding for five hours on low.

Nutrition Info: Per Serving: 206 calories, 8.7g protein, 33.1g carbohydrates, 5g fat, 2.3g fiber, 20mg cholesterol, 173mg sodium, 437mg potassium

French Breakfast Pudding

Servings: 4

Cooking Time: 1 Hour And 30 Minutes

Ingredients:

- 3 egg yolks
- 6 ounces double cream
- 1 teaspoon vanilla extract
- 2 tablespoons caster sugar

Directions:

1. Whisk the sugar and egg yolks together thoroughly in a bowl.
2. Add the cream and vanilla extract, whisk well, and pour the mixture into the four ramekins.
3. Set them in the Crock Pot, fill it with water, cover it, and cook on
4. High for one hour and thirty minutes.
5. Before serving, set aside to cool.

Nutrition Info: calories 261, fat 5, fiber 6, carbs 15, protein 2

Salami Eggs

Servings: 4

Cooking Time: 2.5 Hours

Ingredients:

- 4 oz salami, sliced
- 4 eggs
- 1 teaspoon butter, melted
- 1 tablespoon chives, chopped

Directions:

1. Pour the melted butter into the crock pot.
2. The eggs are broken inside. Salami and chives are then added to the eggs.
3. Cook them for 2.5 hours on high with the lid closed.

Nutrition Info: Per Serving: 146 calories, 9.1g protein, 0.9g carbohydrates, 11.6g fat, 0g fiber, 186mg cholesterol, 392mg sodium, 115mg potassium

Peach, Vanilla And Oats Mix

Servings: 2

Cooking Time: 8 Hours

Ingredients:

- ½ cup steel cut oats
- 2 cups almond milk
- ½ cup peaches, pitted and roughly chopped
- ½ teaspoon vanilla extract
- 1 teaspoon cinnamon powder

Directions:

1. Mix the oats, almond milk, peaches, and other ingredients in your Crock Pot; stir; cover; and cook on low for 8 hours.
2. Serve immediately for breakfast after dividing into bowls.

Nutrition Info: calories 261, fat 5, fiber 8, carbs 18, protein 6

Raspberry Chia Porridge

Servings: 4
Cooking Time: 4 Hours
Ingredients:
- 1 cup raspberry
- 3 tablespoons maple syrup
- 1 cup chia seeds
- 4 cups of milk

Directions:
1. Chia seeds and milk should be combined in a slow cooker and left to simmer for four hours. Blend the raspberries, maple syrup, and other ingredients in the meantime until smooth.
2. Transfer the cooked chia porridge to the serving bowls, then top with the blended raspberry mixture.

Nutrition Info: Per Serving: 315 calories, 13.1g protein, 37.7g carbohydrates, 13.9g fat, 11.7g fiber, 20mg cholesterol, 121mg sodium, 332mg potassium

Smoked Salmon Omelet

Servings: 4
Cooking Time: 2 Hours
Ingredients:
- 4 oz smoked salmon, sliced
- 5 eggs, beaten
- 1 teaspoon ground coriander
- 1 teaspoon butter, melted

Directions:
1. Melted butter should be rubbed onto the crock pot's bottom.
2. Afterward, combine eggs with ground coriander and add the mixture to the crock pot.
   After adding the smoked salmon, cover the pan.
3. For two hours, cook the omelet on high.

Nutrition Info: Per Serving: 120 calories, 12.1g protein, 0.4g carbohydrates, 7.7g fat, 0g fiber, 214mg cholesterol, 651mg sodium, 124mg potassium

Breakfast Monkey Bread

Servings: 6
Cooking Time: 6 Hours
Ingredients:
- 10 oz biscuit rolls
- 1 tablespoon ground cardamom
- 1 tablespoon sugar
- 2 tablespoons coconut oil
- 1 egg, beaten

Directions:
1. Roughly chop the cookie roll.
2. Combine sugar and cardamom powder.

3. Get the coconut oil to melt.
4. Put the 12 parts of chopped biscuit rolls in the Crock Pot in a single layer and top with the remaining 12 parts of the cinnamon mixture and the melted coconut oil.
5. The remaining biscuit roll chops are then placed on top, and the cardamom mixture and coconut oil are added.
6. After that, apply an egg wash to the bread and cover the pan.
7. For six hours on high, prepare the dinner.
8. The bread should be well-cooked.

Nutrition Info: Per Serving: 178 calories, 6.1g protein, 26.4g carbohydrates, 7g fat, 2g fiber, 27mg cholesterol, 238mg sodium, 21mg potassium.

Kale Cups

Servings: 4
Cooking Time: 2.5 Hours
Ingredients:
- 1 cup kale, chopped
- 4 eggs, beaten
- 1 teaspoon olive oil
- 1 teaspoon chili powder
- ½ cup Cheddar cheese, shredded

Directions:

1. Kale, eggs, olive oil, and chili powder are combined. Place the mixture in the ramekins, then sprinkle the cheese on top with Cheddar.
2. In the crock pot, put the ramekins.
3. Cook the meal for 2.5 hours on high with the lid closed.

Nutrition Info: Per Serving: 140 calories, 9.6g protein, 2.6g carbohydrates, 10.3g fat, 0.5g fiber, 179mg cholesterol, 163mg sodium, 168mg potassium

Sweet Quinoa

Servings: 4
Cooking Time: 3 Hours
Ingredients:
- 1 cup quinoa
- ¼ cup dates, chopped
- 3 cups of water
- 1 apricot, chopped
- ½ teaspoon ground nutmeg

Directions:

1. In the slow cooker, combine the quinoa, dates, and apricots.
2. Mix the ingredients after adding the ground nutmeg. Cook it for three hours on high.

Nutrition Info: Per Serving: 194 calories, 6.4g protein, 36.7g carbohydrates, 2.8g fat, 4.1g fiber, 0mg cholesterol, 8g sodium, 338mg potassium.

Leek Bake

Servings: 3
Cooking Time: 8 Hours
Ingredients:

- 2 cups leek, chopped
- 3 oz Cheddar cheese, shredded
- ¼ cup ground chicken
- 1 teaspoon dried thyme
- ½ cup chicken stock

Directions:

1. Fill the crock pot with the chicken stock.
2. Add the leek to the chicken stock along with the ground chicken and dried thyme.
3. Cheddar cheese should then be sprinkled on top, followed by the lid.
4. For eight hours, bake the leeks on low heat.

Nutrition Info: Per Serving: 175 calories, 11.5g protein, 9.1g carbohydrates, 10.6g fat, 1.2g fiber, 40mg cholesterol, 325mg sodium, 168mg potassium.

Milk Pudding

Servings: 2
Cooking Time: 7 Hours
Ingredients:

- 1 cup milk
- 3 eggs, beaten
- 2 tablespoons cornstarch
- 1 teaspoon vanilla extract
- 1 tablespoon white sugar

Directions:

1. Combine milk, cornstarch, and eggs.
   Add white sugar and vanilla extract after smoothing out the mixture.
   Place the Crock Pot's lid on after adding the liquid.
2. Cook it for seven hours on low.

Nutrition Info: Per Serving: 214 calories, 12.3g protein, 20.1g carbohydrates, 9.1g fat, 9.7g fiber, 0.1mg cholesterol, 151mg sodium, 162mg potassium.

Mocha Latte Quinoa Mix

Servings: 4
Cooking Time: 6 Hours
Ingredients:

- 1 cup hot coffee
- 1 cup quinoa
- 1 cup coconut water
- ¼ cup chocolate chips
- ½ cup coconut cream

Directions:

1. Quinoa cooked in a Crock Pot with coffee, coconut water, and chocolate chips for 6 hours on low.
2. Mix, portion into bowls, top with coconut cream, and serve as breakfast.

Nutrition Info: calories 251, fat 4, fiber 7, carbs 15, protein 4

Raisins And Rice Pudding

Servings: 4
Cooking Time: 6 Hours
Ingredients:

- 1 cup long-grain rice
- cups organic almond milk
- 2 tablespoons cornstarch
- 1 teaspoon vanilla extract
- 2 tablespoons raisins, chopped

Directions:

1. Carefully combine all the ingredients in the crock pot. The pudding will then cook on low for 6 hours with the lid closed.

Nutrition Info: Per Serving: 238 calories, 4.1g protein, 49.4g carbohydrates, 1.9g fat, 0.8g fiber, 0mg cholesterol, 91mg sodium, 89mg potassium

Breakfast Meat Rolls

Servings: 12
Cooking Time: 4.5 Hours
Ingredients:

- 1-pound puff pastry
- 1 cup ground pork
- 1 tablespoon garlic, diced
- 1 egg, beaten
- 1 tablespoon sesame oil

Directions:

1. The puff pastry is rolled up. Afterward, combine eggs, garlic, and ground pork.

Spread the ground meat mixture over the puff pastry and roll.

2. Rolls of puff pastry were cut into smaller rolls.
   Sesame oil is then sprinkled over the rolls.
3. In the Crock Pot, arrange the meat rolls, then secure the lid.
   On high, prepare breakfast for 4.5 hours.

Nutrition Info: Per Serving: 244 calories, 4.9g protein, 17.3g carbohydrates, 17.2g fat, 0.6g fiber, 20mg cholesterol, 106mg sodium, 31mg potassium.

Seafood Eggs

Servings: 4
Cooking Time: 2.5 Hours
Ingredients:

- 4 eggs, beaten
- 2 tablespoons cream cheese
- 1 teaspoon Italian seasonings
- 6 oz shrimps, peeled
- 1 teaspoon olive oil

Directions:

1. Combining cream cheese and eggs
2. Add shrimp and Italian seasonings.

3. The egg mixture is then added after lightly oiling the ramekins.
4. Put the ramekins in the slow cooker.
5. For 2.5 hours on high, cook the eggs.

Nutrition Info: Per Serving: 144 calories, 15.6g protein, 1.3g carbohydrates, 8.4g fat, 0g fiber, 260mg cholesterol, 181mg sodium, 138mg potassium

Peach Puree

Servings: 2
Cooking Time: 7 Hours
Ingredients:
- 2 cups peaches, chopped
- 1 tablespoon sugar
- 1 teaspoon ground cinnamon
- ¼ cup of water

Directions:
1. Place each ingredient in the slow cooker.
2. Cook them on low for seven hours with the lid on.
3. Then use the immersion blender to create the puree.
4. For up to a day, keep the puree in the refrigerator.

Nutrition Info: Per Serving: 84 calories, 1.5g protein, 20.9g

carbohydrates, 0.4g fat, 2.9g fiber, 0mg cholesterol, 1mg sodium, 290mg potassium

Salmon Frittata

Servings: 3
Cooking Time: 3 Hours And 40 Minutes
Ingredients:
- 4 eggs, whisked
- ½ teaspoon olive oil
- 2 tablespoons green onions, chopped
- Salt and black pepper to the taste
- 4 ounces smoked salmon, chopped

Directions:
1. In your Crock Pot, drizzle some oil, add the eggs, salt, and pepper, stir, then cover and cook on low for three hours.
2. Toss the salmon and green onions in, cover, and simmer on low for an additional 40 minutes before dividing among plates.
3. Serve immediately as breakfast.

Nutrition Info: calories 220, fat 10, fiber 2, carbs 15, protein 7

Appetizers Recipes

Chipotle Bbq Sausage Bites

Servings: 10
Cooking Time: 2 1/4 Hours
Ingredients:

- 3 pounds small smoked sausages
- 1 cup BBQ sauce
- 2 chipotle peppers in adobo sauce
- 1 tablespoon tomato paste
- 1/4 cup white wine
- Salt and pepper to taste

Directions:

1. Place each ingredient in the crock pot.
2. If necessary, season with salt and pepper and cover with a lid.
3. Cook for two hours on the highest setting.
4. The sausage bites can be served warm or cold.

Bacon Chicken Sliders

Servings: 8
Cooking Time: 4 1/2 Hours
Ingredients:

- 2 pounds ground chicken
- 1 egg
- 1/2 cup breadcrumbs
- 1 shallot, chopped
- Salt and pepper to taste
- 8 bacon slices

Directions:

1. In a bowl, combine the chicken, egg, breadcrumbs, and shallot. Give it a good mix after adding salt and pepper to taste. Create tiny sliders, then cover each with a bacon slice. Sliders should be put in a crock pot.
2. Make sure to turn them over once while cooking, then cover with the lid and cook on high for 4 hours.
Offer them something hot.

Boiled Peanuts With Skin On

Servings: 8
Cooking Time: 7 1/4 Hours
Ingredients:

- 2 pounds uncooked, whole peanuts
- 1/2 cup salt
- 4 cups water

Directions:

1. Place each ingredient in the crock pot.
2. 7 hours on low heat with a cover over the food.
3. Drain, then let the food cool completely before serving.

Maple Syrup Glazed Carrots

Servings: 8
Cooking Time: 6 1/4 Hours
Ingredients:

- 3 pounds baby carrots
- 4 tablespoons butter, melted
- 3 tablespoons maple syrup
- 1/8 teaspoon pumpkin pie spices
- 1 teaspoon salt

Directions:

1. The remaining ingredients should be added to the crock pot along with the baby carrots.
2. The carrots should be evenly coated after mixing.
3. Cook for six hours with a lid on the low setting.
4. Carrots can be served warm or cold.

Bacon Baked Potatoes

Servings: 8
Cooking Time: 3 1/4 Hours
Ingredients:

- 3 pounds new potatoes, halved
- 8 slices bacon, chopped
- 1 teaspoon dried rosemary
- 1/4 cup chicken stock
- Salt and pepper to taste

Directions:

1. Add the bacon to a skillet that has been heated over medium heat. until crisp, cook.

2. Put the potatoes in the slow cooker. Mix in the rosemary, salt, pepper, and bacon bits and fat until everything is evenly distributed.
3. Add the stock, then cook it for three hours on high heat.
4. Warm potatoes should be served.

Bacon New Potatoes

Servings: 6
Cooking Time: 3 1/4 Hours
Ingredients:

- 3 pounds new potatoes, washed and halved
- 12 slices bacon, chopped
- 2 tablespoons white wine
- Salt and pepper to taste
- 1 rosemary sprig

Directions:

1. In your crock pot, add the potatoes, wine, and rosemary. Chop some bacon and sprinkle with salt and pepper to taste. Cook for three hours on high.
2. Warm potatoes should be served.

Cheesy Beef Dip

Servings: 8
Cooking Time: 3 1/4 Hours
Ingredients:

- 2 pounds ground beef
- 1 pound grated Cheddar

- 1/2 cup cream cheese
- 1/2 cup white wine
- 1 poblano pepper, chopped

Directions:

1. In a crockpot, combine all the ingredients.
2. Cook for three hours on high.
3. Serve hot, if possible.

French Onion Dip

Servings: 10
Cooking Time: 4 1/4 Hours
Ingredients:

- 4 large onions, chopped
- 2 tablespoons olive oil
- 1 tablespoon butter
- 1 1/2 cups sour cream
- 1 pinch nutmeg
- Salt and pepper to taste

Directions:

1. In a crock pot, mix the onions, butter, salt, pepper, and nutmeg.
   Cook for 4 hours with the cover on high.
2. Once finished, let the dish cool before adding the sour cream and seasoning with salt and pepper to taste.
3. Give the dip a quick serving.

Sausage Dip

Servings: 8
Cooking Time: 6 1/4 Hours
Ingredients:

- 1 pound fresh pork sausages
- 1 pound spicy pork sausages
- 1 cup cream cheese
- 1 can diced tomatoes
- 2 poblano peppers, chopped

Directions:

1. In a crockpot, combine all the ingredients.
2. Cook for six hours at a low temperature.
3. Serve hot or cold.

Bourbon Glazed Sausages

Servings: 10
Cooking Time: 4 1/4 Hours
Ingredients:

- 3 pounds small sausage links
- 1/2 cup apricot preserves
- 1/4 cup maple syrup
- 2 tablespoons Bourbon

Directions:

1. Place each ingredient in the crock pot.
2. Cook for 4 hours on low heat with the lid on.
3. In either case, serve the glazed sausages with cocktail sticks.

Bacon Wrapped Dates

Servings: 8
Cooking Time: 1 3/4 Hours
Ingredients:

- 16 dates, pitted
- 16 almonds
- 16 slices bacon

Directions:

1. Fill an almond with each date.
2. Place the dates that have been wrapped in bacon in your slow cooker.
3. Cook on high for 1 1/4 hours while covering the pot with its lid.
4. Serve hot or cold.

Cranberry Baked Brie

Servings: 6
Cooking Time: 2 1/4 Hours
Ingredients:

- 1 wheel of Brie
- 1/2 cup cranberry sauce
- 1/2 teaspoon dried thyme

Directions:

1. By spoonfuls, add the cranberry sauce to the crock pot.

2. The Brie cheese should be placed on top after the herbs.
3. Cook for two hours on low heat, covered.
4. Warm cheese is best served with tortilla chips or breadsticks.

Bacon Wrapped Chicken Livers

Servings: 6
Cooking Time: 3 1/2 Hours
Ingredients:

- 2 pounds chicken livers
- Bacon slices as needed

Directions:

1. Place all the chicken livers in the crock pot after wrapping each one with a piece of bacon.
2. 3 hours of cooking at a high heat
3. Serve hot or cold.

Beef, Pork & Lamb Recipes

Blanked Hot Dogs

Servings: 4
Cooking Time: 4 Hours
Ingredients:
- 4 mini (cocktail) pork sausages
- 1 teaspoon cumin seeds
- 1 tablespoon olive oil
- 1 egg, beaten
- 4 oz puff pastry

Directions:
1. Puff pastry should be rolled and then cut into strips.
2. The pork sausages should be placed on each strip.
3. Brush eggs on the puff pastry before rolling.
4. Cumin seeds are then sprinkled on top of the hot dogs.
5. From the inside, rub some olive oil on the crock pot.
6. Close the lid after adding the blanked hot dogs.
7. Cook them for four hours on high.

Nutrition Info: Per Serving: 225 calories, 4.4g protein, 14.1g carbohydrates, 16.9g fat, 0.6g fiber, 41mg cholesterol, 120mg sodium, 42mg potassium

Beef Brisket In Orange Juice

Servings: 4
Cooking Time: 5 Hours
Ingredients:
- 1 cup of orange juice
- 2 cups of water
- 2 tablespoons butter
- 12 oz beef brisket
- ½ teaspoon salt

Directions:
1. Melt the butter in the skillet.
2. Place the beef brisket in the melted butter and roast for 3 minutes on each side over high heat.
3. After adding salt, place the meat in the crock pot.
4. Add water and orange juice.
5. Put the lid on the pot and cook the meat for 5 hours on high.

Nutrition Info: Per Serving: 237 calories, 26.3g protein, 6.5g carbohydrates, 11.2g fat, 0.1g fiber, 91mg cholesterol, 392mg sodium, 470mg potassium.

Tenderloin Steaks With Red Wine And Mushrooms

Servings: 4
Cooking Time: 12 Hours
Ingredients:
- 4 pounds beef tenderloin steaks
- Salt and pepper to taste

- 1 package Portobello mushrooms, sliced
- 1 cup dry red wine
- 2 tablespoons butter

Directions:

1. Put all the ingredients in the slow cooker.
2. Make a thorough stir.
3. Cook for 12 hours on low or 10 hours on high with the lid securely on.

Nutrition Info: Calories per serving: 415; Carbohydrates:7.2 g; Protein:30.3 g; Fat: 27.4g; Sugar: 0g; Sodium: 426mg; Fiber:3.8 g

Beef Sausages In Maple Syrup

Servings: 4
Cooking Time: 5 Hours
Ingredients:

- 1-pound beef sausages
- ½ cup maple syrup
- 3 tablespoons butter
- 1 teaspoon ground cumin
- ¼ cup of water

Directions:

1. Place the butter in the skillet and let it melt.
2. The melted butter should now be added to the crock pot.
3. Cumin, maple syrup, and water are added. Smoothen the liquid by stirring it.

4. Seal the lid after adding the beef sausages.
5. Cook the food for five hours on high.

Nutrition Info: Per Serving: 630 calories, 15.8 g protein, 29.7g carbohydrates, 50g fat, 0.1g fiber, 103mg cholesterol, 979mg sodium, 307mg potassium.

Cayenne Pepper Strips

Servings: 4
Cooking Time: 4 Hours
Ingredients:

- 1-pound pork sirloin, cut into strips
- 1 teaspoon cayenne pepper
- 2 tablespoons ketchup
- 1 tablespoon avocado oil
- 1 cup of water

Directions:

1. Combine ketchup, cayenne, and avocado oil.
2. The pork strips are then carefully brushed with the ketchup mixture and placed in the crock pot.
3. Close the cover after adding water.
4. For four hours, cook the meat on high.

Nutrition Info: Per Serving: 204 calories, 23.3g protein, 2.3g carbohydrates, 10.6g fat, 0.3g fiber, 80mg cholesterol, 151mg sodium, 49mg potassium

Crockpot Cheeseburgers Casserole

Servings: 4
Cooking Time: 8 Hours
Ingredients:
- 1 white onion, chopped
- 1 ½ pounds lean ground beef
- 2 tablespoons mustard
- 1 teaspoon dried basil leaves
- 2 cups cheddar cheese

Directions:
1. For three minutes, sauté ground beef and white onions in a heated skillet over medium heat. Stir continuously until golden.
2. Add basil leaves and mustard after being transferred to the slow cooker. Add salt and pepper to taste.
   top with cheese.
3. Cook for 8 hours on low and 6 hours on high with the lid closed.

Nutrition Info: Calories per serving: 472; Carbohydrates: 3g; Protein: 32.7g; Fat: 26.2g; Sugar: 0g; Sodium: 429mg; Fiber: 2.4g

Beef Casserole

Servings: 5
Cooking Time: 7 Hours

Ingredients:
- 7 oz ground beef
- 1 cup Cheddar cheese, shredded
- ½ cup cream
- 1 teaspoon Italian seasonings
- ½ cup broccoli, chopped

Directions:
1. Italian seasonings are combined with ground beef, then added to the crock pot.
2. Cheese and broccoli are placed on top of the meat.
3. After that, add the cream to the casserole mixture and cover it.
4. For seven hours, cook the casserole on low.

Nutrition Info: Per Serving: 186 calories, 18.1g protein, 1.7g carbohydrates, 11.6g fat, 0.2g fiber, 64mg cholesterol, 178mg sodium, 220mg potassium.

Seasoned Poached Pork Belly

Servings: 4
Cooking Time: 4 Hours
Ingredients:
- 10 oz pork belly
- 1 teaspoon minced garlic
- 1 teaspoon ginger paste
- ¼ cup apple cider vinegar
- 1 cup of water

Directions:

1. Garlic paste and minced garlic should be applied to the pork belly.
   After that, add apple cider vinegar and put it in the crock pot.
2. Close the cover after adding water.
3. For four hours on high, cook the pork belly.
4. The cooked pork belly is then sliced and topped with warm Crock Pot sauce.

Nutrition Info: Per Serving: 333 calories, 32.8g protein, 0.7g carbohydrates, 19.1g fat, 0.1g fiber, 82mg cholesterol, 1148mg sodium, 20mg potassium

Pesto Pork Chops

Servings: 4
Cooking Time: 8 Hours
Ingredients:
- 4 pork chops
- 4 teaspoons pesto sauce
- 4 tablespoons butter

Directions:
1. Brush pesto sauce on the pork chops.
2. Butter is placed in the crock pot.
3. Close the cover after adding the pork chops.
4. The beef for eight hours on low heat.

5. After that, serve the cooked pork chops on top of the Crock Pot butter-pesto gravy.

Nutrition Info: Per Serving: 380 calories, 18.6g protein, 0.3g carbohydrates, 33.6g fat, 0.1g fiber, 101mg cholesterol, 89mg sodium, 279mg potassium

Bacon Beef Strips

Servings: 4
Cooking Time: 5 Hours
Ingredients:
- 1-pound beef tenderloin, cut into strips
- 4 oz bacon, sliced
- 1 teaspoon salt
- ½ teaspoon ground black pepper
- ½ cup of water

Directions:
1. Add salt and freshly ground black pepper to the meat.
2. After that, place each beef strip in the crock pot after wrapping it with bacon slices.
3. Close the cover after adding water.
4. Cook the food for five hours on high.

Nutrition Info: Per Serving: 258 calories,28.9g protein, 0.4g carbohydrates, 14.8g fat, 0.1g fiber, 90mg cholesterol, 869mg sodium, 379mg potassium.

Basil Beef

Servings: 4
Cooking Time: 4 Hours
Ingredients:

- 1-pound beef loin, chopped
- 2 tablespoons dried basil
- 2 tablespoons butter
- ½ cup of water
- 1 teaspoon salt

Directions:

1. Place the butter in the skillet and let it melt.
2. The beef loin is then combined with dried basil and smothered in hot butter.
3. After roasting the meat for two minutes on each side, place it in the crock pot.
4. Add water and salt.
5. Beef should be cooked for 4 hours on high with the lid closed.

Nutrition Info: Per Serving: 220 calories, 21g protein, 1.4g carbohydrates, 13.9g fat, 0g fiber, 76mg cholesterol, 1123mg sodium, 6mg potassium.

Kebab Cubes

Servings: 4
Cooking Time: 5 Hours
Ingredients:

- 1 teaspoon curry powder
- 1 teaspoon dried mint
- 1 teaspoon cayenne pepper
- ½ cup plain yogurt
- 1-pound beef tenderloin, cubed

Directions:

1. Mix the beef cubes, curry powder, dried mint, cayenne pepper, and plain yogurt in a mixing bowl.
2. After that, put the mixture in the crock pot. If there is not enough liquid, add water and cover the container.
3. Cook the food for five hours on high.

Nutrition Info: Per Serving: 259 calories, 34.7g protein, 2.7g carbohydrates, 10.9g fat, 0.3g fiber, 106mg cholesterol, 89mg sodium, 495mg potassium.

Easy Crockpot Pulled Pork

Servings: 4
Cooking Time: 12 Hours
Ingredients:

- 4 pork shoulder, trimmed from excess fat
- 1 small onion, sliced
- Salt and pepper to taste
- 1 cup water
- 1 teaspoon rosemary

Directions:

1. Put all the ingredients in the slow cooker.
2. Cook for 12 hours on low or 8 hours on high.

3. After cooking, shred the meat using forks.

Nutrition Info: Calories per serving: 533; Carbohydrates: 2g; Protein: 47.2g; Fat: 32.3g; Sugar: 0g; Sodium: 629mg; Fiber: 1.4g

Thyme Beef

Servings: 2
Cooking Time: 5 Hours
Ingredients:
- 8 oz beef sirloin, chopped
- 1 tablespoon dried thyme
- 1 tablespoon olive oil
- ½ cup of water
- 1 teaspoon salt

Directions:
1. Well, warm up the skillet.
2. Then combine the meat with olive oil and dried thyme.
3. The meat should be roasted in a heated pan for two minutes on each side.
4. Then place the meat in the slow cooker.
5. Add water and salt.
6. Cook the food for five hours on high.

Nutrition Info: Per Serving: 274 calories, 34.5g protein, 0.9g carbohydrates, 14.2g fat, 0.5g fiber, 101mg cholesterol, 1240mg sodium, 469mg potassium.

Roast With Pepperoncini

Servings: 4
Cooking Time: 8 Hrs.
Ingredients:
- 5 lbs. beef chuck roast
- 1 tbsp soy sauce
- 10 pepperoncini's
- 1 cup beef stock
- 2 tbsp butter, melted

Directions:
1. Place the beef roast in the Crock Pot insert along with the remaining ingredients.
2. Put the lid on the cooker and select the low setting for 8 hours of cooking time.
3. With the aid of two forks, shred the cooked meat and put it back in the cooker.
4. Stir gently, then warmly serve.

Nutrition Info: Per Serving: Calories: 362, Total Fat: 4g, Fiber: 8g, Total Carbs: 17g, Protein: 17g

Naked Beef Enchilada In A Crockpot

Servings: 4
Cooking Time: 6 Hours
Ingredients:
- 1-pound ground beef
- 2 tablespoons enchilada spice mix
- 1 cup cauliflower florets
- 2 cups Mexican cheese blend, grated

- ¼ cup cilantro, chopped

Directions:
1. The ground beef should be cooked for three minutes over medium heat in a skillet.
2. Add the cauliflower and enchilada spice mix to the crockpot after the transfer.
3. To combine, stir.
4. On top, sprinkle the Mexican cheese mixture.
5. Cook for six hours on low or four hours on high.
6. On top, sprinkle some cilantro.

Nutrition Info: Calories per serving: 481; Carbohydrates: 1g; Protein: 35.1g; Fat: 29.4g; Sugar: 0g; Sodium: 536mg; Fiber:0 g

Garlic Pork Ribs

Servings: 3
Cooking Time: 5.5 Hours
Ingredients:
- 8 oz pork ribs, chopped
- 1 teaspoon garlic powder
- 1 teaspoon avocado oil
- ½ teaspoon salt
- ½ cup of water

Directions:
1. The skillet should be heated up.
2. After that, add the pork ribs to the heated skillet and add the garlic powder and avocado oil.

3. The ribs should be roasted for 3 minutes on each side, or until light brown.
4. After that, put the pork ribs in the slow cooker and season with salt.
5. Cook the ribs for five hours on high after adding water.

Nutrition Info: Per Serving: 212 calories, 20.2g protein, 0.8g carbohydrates, 13.6g fat, 0.2g fiber, 78mg cholesterol, 433mg sodium, 233mg potassium.

Pepsi Pork Tenderloin

Servings: 4
Cooking Time: 6 Hours
Ingredients:
- 1-pound pork tenderloin
- 1 cup Pepsi
- 1 teaspoon cumin seeds
- 1 teaspoon olive oil
- 2 tablespoons soy sauce

Directions:
1. Put the rough-cut pork tenderloin in the mixing bowl.
2. Olive oil, soy sauce, Pepsi, and cumin seeds should be added.
3. Allow the meat to marinate for 30 minutes.
4. After that, add all of the Pepsi liquid to the crock pot along with the meat, and then secure the lid.

5. For six hours, cook the meat on low heat.

Nutrition Info: Per Serving: 179 calories, 30.3g protein, 0.8g carbohydrates, 5.3g fat, 0.1g fiber,83mg cholesterol, 523mg sodium, 514mg potassium

Tender Butter Knuckle

Servings: 4
Cooking Time: 8 Hours
Ingredients:
- 1-pound pork knuckle
- 1/3 cup butter
- 1 teaspoon dried rosemary
- 1 teaspoon dried thyme
- ½ cup of coconut milk

Directions:
1. Blend the butter with the dried thyme and rosemary.
2. Put the pork knuckle in the crock pot after giving it a little massage.
3. After adding coconut milk, cover the pot.
4. For eight hours, cook the food on low.

Nutrition Info: Per Serving: 448 calories, 33.2g protein, 2g carbohydrates, 34.1g fat, 0.9g fiber, 137mg cholesterol, 195mg sodium, 543mg potassium

Chili Beef Sausages

Servings: 5

Cooking Time: 4 Hours
Ingredients:
- 1-pound beef sausages
- 1 tablespoon olive oil
- ¼ cup of water
- 1 teaspoon chili powder

Directions:
1. Fill the crock pot with olive oil.
2. After that, add chili powder and place the beef sausages in the crock pot.
3. Close the cover after adding water.
4. For four hours on high, cook the beef sausages.

Nutrition Info: Per Serving: 385 calories, 12.6g protein, 2.7g carbohydrates, 35.8g fat, 0.2g fiber, 64mg cholesterol, 736mg sodium, 182mg potassium.

Apple Pork

Servings: 4
Cooking Time: 8 Hours
Ingredients:
- 1-pound pork tenderloin, chopped
- 1 teaspoon ground cinnamon
- 1 tablespoon maple syrup
- 1 cup apples, chopped
- 1 cup of water

Directions:

1. Apples are combined with cinnamon powder and placed in a slow cooker.
2. Pork tenderloin, maple syrup, and water are added.
   Cook the food on low for 8 hours with the lid shut.

Nutrition Info: Per Serving: 206 calories, 29.9g protein, 11.5g carbohydrates, 4.1g fat, 1.7g fiber, 83mg cholesterol, 67mg sodium, 550mg potassium

Jamaican Pork Shoulder

Servings: 12
Cooking Time: 7 Hrs.
Ingredients:
- ½ cup beef stock
- 1 tbsp olive oil
- ¼ cup keto Jamaican spice mix
- 4 lbs. pork shoulder

Directions:
1. Add the pork, Jamaican spice blend, and remaining ingredients to the crock pot.
2. Put the lid on the cooker and select the low setting for 7 hours of cooking time.
3. Warm the roast before slicing it.

Nutrition Info: Per Serving: Calories: 400, Total Fat: 6g, Fiber: 7g, Total Carbs: 10g, Protein: 25g

Chili Beef Strips

Servings: 4
Cooking Time: 6 Hours
Ingredients:
- 1-pound beef loin, cut into strips
- 1 chili pepper, chopped
- 2 tablespoons coconut oil
- 1 teaspoon salt
- 1 teaspoon chili powder

Directions:
1. Sprinkle salt and chili powder on the beef strips.
2. After that, add the chili pepper to the slow cooker.
3. Beef strips and coconut oil are added.
4. Cook the food on low for 6 hours with the lid securely on.

Nutrition Info: Per Serving: 267 calories, 30.4g protein, 0.5g carbohydrates, 16.4g fat, 0.3g fiber, 81mg cholesterol, 650mg sodium, 401mg potassium.

Beef-stuffed Peppers

Servings: 8
Cooking Time: 5 Hours
Ingredients:
- 1-pound lean ground beef
- 1 can tomatoes and chilies
- 1 teaspoon cumin
- 8 medium sweet peppers, top and seeds removed
- 2 cups Mexican cheese blend

Directions:
1. Add the ground beef to a skillet that is heated over medium heat.
2. For 3 minutes, stir until golden.
3. The cumin and tomatoes. Cut the heat and let it cool.
   Fill the sweet peppers with the beef mixture. Add the Mexican cheese mixture on top.
4. Place the contents inside, then secure the lid.
5. Cook for five hours on low or three hours on high.

Nutrition Info: Calories per serving: 301; Carbohydrates: 2.5g; Protein:29 g; Fat: 14g; Sugar:0.3 g; Sodium: 797mg; Fiber: 3g

Taco Pork

Servings: 5
Cooking Time: 5 Hours
Ingredients:
- 1-pound pork shoulder, chopped
- 1 tablespoon taco seasonings
- 1 tablespoon lemon juice
- 1 cup of water

Directions:
1. Pork shoulder is combined with taco seasoning and placed in a slow cooker.
2. Cook it for 5 hours on high after adding water.
3. After that, put the cooked meat in the bowl and use a fork to gently shred it.
4. Shake gently while adding lemon juice.

Nutrition Info: Per Serving: 274 calories, 21.1g protein, 1.7g carbohydrates, 19.4g fat, 0g fiber, 82mg cholesterol, 232mg sodium, 303mg potassium

Cheesy Pork Casserole

Servings: 4
Cooking Time: 10 Hours
Ingredients:
- 4 pork chops, bones removed and sliced
- 1 cauliflower head, cut into florets
- 1 cup chicken broth
- 1 teaspoon rosemary
- 2 cups cheddar cheese

Directions:
1. Place the cauliflower florets and pork chop slices in the slow cooker.
2. Pour in the chicken broth and rosemary.To taste, add salt and pepper to the food.
3. Top with cheddar cheese.
4. Cook for 10 hours on low with the lid on.

Nutrition Info: Calories per serving: 417; Carbohydrates: 7g; Protein: 32.1g; Fat: 26.2g; Sugar: 0; Sodium: 846mg; Fiber: 5.3g

Chili Crockpot Brisket

Servings: 4
Cooking Time: 12 Hours
Ingredients:

- 4 pounds beef brisket
- 1 bottle chili sauce
- Salt and pepper to taste
- 1 cup onion, chopped
- 1/8 cup water

Directions:

1. Put all the ingredients in the slow cooker.
   Make a thorough stir.
2. Cook for 12 hours on low or 10 hours on high with the lid securely on.

Nutrition Info: Calories per serving: 634; Carbohydrates: 2.1g; Protein: 30.2g; Fat: 45.4g; Sugar:0 g; Sodium: 835mg; Fiber: 1.4g

Crockpot Pork Roast

Servings: 4
Cooking Time: 12 Hours
Ingredients:

- 1-pound pork loin roast, bones removed
- 3 tablespoons olive oil
- 1 teaspoon thyme leaves

- 1 teaspoon marjoram leaves
- ½ tablespoon dry mustard

Directions:

1. Foil should be used to line the crockpot's bottom.
2. In a bowl, combine all the ingredients. Massage the spices into the pork to cover every surface.
3. Cook for 12 hours on low or 8 hours on high in a slow cooker.

Nutrition Info: Calories per serving: 414; Carbohydrates: 0.8g; Protein: 52.2; Fat: 37.1g; Sugar:0 g; Sodium: 724mg; Fiber: 0g

Crockpot Moroccan Beef

Servings: 8
Cooking Time: 10 Hours
Ingredients:

- 2 pounds beef roast, cut into strips
- ½ cup onions, sliced
- 4 tablespoons garam masala
- 1 teaspoon salt
- ½ cup bone broth

Directions:

1. All ingredients should be put in the crockpot.
2. Make a thorough stir.
3. Cook for 8 hours on high or 10 hours on low while covering the pan.

Nutrition Info: Calories per serving: 310; Carbohydrates: 0.7g; Protein: 30.3g; Fat: 25.5g; Sugar: 0g; Sodium: 682mg; Fiber: 0.5g

Bbq Beer Beef Tenderloin

Servings: 4
Cooking Time: 10 Hours
Ingredients:

- ¼ cup beer
- 1-pound beef tenderloin
- ½ cup BBQ sauce
- 1 teaspoon fennel seeds
- 1 teaspoon olive oil

Directions:

1. Combine beer, fennel seeds, and olive oil with the BBQ sauce.
2. Fill the crock pot with the liquid.
3. Close the lid after adding the beef tenderloin.
4. For ten hours, cook the food on low.

Nutrition Info: Per Serving: 299 calories, 33g protein, 12.1g carbohydrates, 11.7g fat, 0.4g fiber, 104mg cholesterol, 418mg sodium, 482mg potassium.

Poultry Recipes

Sweet Chicken Mash

Servings: 6
Cooking Time: 7 Hours
Ingredients:

- 3 tablespoons maple syrup
- 1-pound ground chicken
- 1 teaspoon dried dill
- 1 cup Cheddar cheese, shredded
- 1 cup of water

Directions:

1. Carefully combine all the ingredients in the crock pot. Cook the mash on low for 7 hours with the lid shut.

Nutrition Info: Per Serving: 246 calories, 26.6g protein, 7g carbohydrates, 11.9g fat, 0g fiber, 87mg cholesterol, 184mg sodium, 229mg potassium.

Chicken Piccata

Servings: 4
Cooking Time: 8 Hours
Ingredients:

- 4 chicken breasts, skin and bones removed
- Salt and pepper to taste
- ¼ cup butter, cubed
- ¼ cup chicken broth
- 1 tablespoon lemon juice

Directions:

1. Put all the ingredients in the slow cooker.
2. Stir everything well to thoroughly combine it..
3. Cook for 8 hours on low or 6 hours on high with the lid securely on.

Nutrition Info: Calories per serving: 265; Carbohydrates:2.3 g; Protein:24 g; Fat: 14g; Sugar: 0g; Sodium:442 mg; Fiber:0 g

Continental Beef Chicken

Servings: 5
Cooking Time: 9 Hours
Ingredients:

- 6 oz. dried beef
- 12 oz. chicken breast, diced
- 7 oz. sour cream
- 1 can onion soup
- 3 tbsp flour

Directions:

1. In the crock pot, distribute half of the dried beef.
2. On top, sprinkle flour, onion soup, sour cream, and chicken breast.
3. On top, distribute the remaining dried beef.
4. Close the cooker's lid and select the low cooking setting for 9 hours.
5. Serve hot.

Nutrition Info: Per Serving: Calories: 285, Total Fat: 15.1g, Fiber: 1g, Total Carbs: 12.56g, Protein: 24g

Orange Chicken

Servings: 4
Cooking Time: 7 Hours
Ingredients:
- 1-pound chicken fillet, roughly chopped
- 4 oranges, peeled, chopped
- 1 cup of water
- 1 teaspoon peppercorns
- 1 onion, diced

Directions:
1. Place the oranges and chicken in the slow cooker.
2. Add water, onions, and peppercorns.
3. Cook the food on low for 7 hours with the lid shut.

Nutrition Info: Per Serving: 314 calories, 34.9g protein, 24.5g carbohydrates, 8.7g fat, 5.2g fiber, 101mg cholesterol, 101mg sodium, 656mg potassium.

Chicken Parm

Servings: 3
Cooking Time: 4 Hours
Ingredients:
- 9 oz chicken fillet
- 1/3 cup cream
- 3 oz Parmesan, grated
- 1 teaspoon olive oil

Directions:
1. Apply olive oil from the inside to the bowl of the crock pot.
2. Next, cut the chicken fillet into slices and put it in the slow cooker.
3. Add some Parmesan and cream on top.
4. Cook the food for 4 hours on high with the lid closed.

Nutrition Info: Per Serving: 283 calories, 33.9g protein, 1.8g carbohydrates, 15.4g fat, 0g fiber, 101mg cholesterol, 345mg sodium, 216mg potassium.

French-style Chicken

Servings: 4
Cooking Time: 7 Hours
Ingredients:
- 1 can onion soup
- 4 chicken drumsticks
- ½ cup celery stalk, chopped
- 1 teaspoon dried tarragon
- ¼ cup white wine

Directions:
1. Mix the ingredients thoroughly before adding them to the crock pot.
2. After that, secure the lid and cook the chicken for 7 hours on low.

Nutrition Info: Per Serving: 127 calories, 15.1g protein, 5.8g

carbohydrates, 3.7g fat, 0.7g fiber, 40mg cholesterol, 688mg sodium, 185mg potassium.

Chicken And Sour Cream

Servings: 4
Cooking Time: 4 Hours
Ingredients:
- 4 chicken thighs
- Salt and black pepper to the taste
- 1 teaspoon onion powder
- ¼ cup sour cream
- 2 tablespoons sweet paprika

Directions:
1. Paprika, salt, pepper, and onion powder should be combined in a bowl and stirred.
2. The chicken pieces should be seasoned with this paprika mixture, added to your Crock Pot, mixed with sour cream, covered, and cooked on high for 4 hours.
3. Serve everything after dividing it among the plates.

Nutrition Info: calories 384, fat 31, fiber 2, carbs 11, protein 33

Rosemary Rotisserie Chicken

Servings: 12
Cooking Time: 12 Hours
Ingredients:
- 1-gallon water
- ¾ cup salt
- ½ cup butter
- 2 tablespoons rosemary and other herbs of your choice
- 1 whole chicken, excess fat removed

Directions:
1. Combine the water, salt, sugar, and herbs in a pot.
2. Salt and sugar must be stirred to dissolve.
3. Completely submerge the chicken and let it rest in the brine for 12 hours in the refrigerator.
4. Tin foil is used to line the crockpot.
5. Place the chicken in the oven and cook for 12 hours on low or 7 hours on high.

Nutrition Info: Calories per serving: 194; Carbohydrates: 1.4g; Protein:20.6 g; Fat:6.2g; Sugar: 0g; Sodium: 562mg; Fiber: 0.9g

Stuffed Chicken Fillets

Servings: 6
Cooking Time: 4 Hours
Ingredients:
- ½ cup green peas, cooked
- ½ cup long-grain rice, cooked
- 16 oz chicken fillets
- 1 cup of water

- 1 teaspoon Italian seasonings

Directions:
1. Cut the chicken fillets horizontally.
2. After that, combine rice and green peas with Italian seasonings.
3. With toothpicks, affix the filled chicken fillet to the rice mixture.
4. Chicken fillets should be placed in a slow cooker.
5. Close the lid after adding water.
6. For four hours, cook the chicken on high.

Nutrition Info: Per Serving: 212 calories, 23.6g protein, 14.2g carbohydrates, 6g fat, 0.8g fiber, 68mg cholesterol, 68mg sodium, 232mg potassium.

Tomato Chicken Sausages

Servings: 4
Cooking Time: 2 Hours
Ingredients:
- 1-pound chicken sausages
- 1 cup tomato juice
- 1 tablespoon dried sage
- 1 teaspoon salt
- 1 teaspoon olive oil

Directions:
1. The skillet's olive oil is well warmed.

2. Add the chicken sausages and cook them over high heat for one minute on each side.
3. After that, put the chicken sausages in the slow cooker.
4. After adding everything else, cover the container.
5. For two hours, cook the chicken sausages on high.

Nutrition Info: Per Serving: 236 calories, 15.3g protein, 10.5g carbohydrates, 13.7g fat, 1.1g fiber, 0mg cholesterol, 1198mg sodium, 145mg potassium.

Creamy Chicken

Servings: 4
Cooking Time: 4 Hrs
Ingredients:
- 4 chicken thighs
- Salt and black pepper to the taste
- 1 tsp onion powder
- ¼ cup sour cream
- 2 tbsp sweet paprika

Directions:
1. To the crock pot, add the chicken, paprika, sour cream, salt, black pepper, and onion powder.
2. Put the cover on the cooker and choose a high cooking mode for 4 hours.
3. Serve hot.

Nutrition Info: Per Serving: Calories: 384, Total Fat: 31g, Fiber: 2g, Total Carbs: 11g, Protein: 33g

Halved Chicken

Servings: 4
Cooking Time: 5 Hours
Ingredients:
- 2-pounds whole chicken, halved
- 1 tablespoon salt
- 1 teaspoon ground black pepper
- 2 tablespoons mayonnaise
- ½ cup of water

Directions:
1. Combine the mayonnaise, salt, and freshly ground black pepper.
2. After applying the mayonnaise mixture, place the chicken halves in the slow cooker.
3. Close the lid after adding water.
4. For five hours on high, cook the chicken.

Nutrition Info: Per Serving: 461 calories, 65.7g protein, 2.1g carbohydrates, 19.3g fat, 1.2g fiber, 0.1mg cholesterol, 1993mg sodium, 559mg potassium.

Spicy Almond-crusted Chicken Nuggets In The Crockpot

Servings: 6
Cooking Time: 8 Hours
Ingredients:
- ¼ cup butter, melted
- 1 ½ cups almond meal
- 1 ½ cups grated parmesan cheese
- 1 ½ pounds boneless chicken breasts, cut into strips
- 2 eggs, beaten

Directions:
1. The crockpot's bottom should be lined with foil.
2. Almond meal and parmesan cheese should be combined.
3. After dipping the chicken strips in the eggs, coat them with the cheese and parmesan mixture.
4. Put it carefully into the slow cooker.
5. Cook for 8 hours on low or 6 hours on high with the lid securely on.

Nutrition Info: Calories per serving: 371; Carbohydrates: 2.5g; Protein:29 g; Fat: 22g; Sugar: 0.8g; Sodium: 527mg; Fiber: 1.4g

Harissa Chicken Breasts

Servings: 6
Cooking Time: 8 Hours
Ingredients:
- 1 tablespoon olive oil

- 1-pound chicken breasts, skin and bones removed
- Salt to taste
- 2 tablespoon Harissa or Sriracha sauce
- 2 tablespoons toasted sesame seeds

Directions:
1. Fill the crockpot with oil.
2. Place the chicken breasts in a line and season with salt and pepper as desired.
3. Add the Sriracha or Harissa sauce and stir. Stir thoroughly to combine everything.
4. Cook for 8 hours on low or 6 hours on high with the lid securely on.
5. Sprinkle toasted sesame seeds on top after cooking.

Nutrition Info: Calories per serving: 167; Carbohydrates: 1.1g; Protein: 16.3g; Fat: 10.6g; Sugar: 0g; Sodium: 632mg; Fiber: 0.6g

Chicken Enchilada

Servings: 10
Cooking Time: 8 Hours
Ingredients:
- 4 ½ cups shredded chicken
- 1 ¼ cup sour cream
- 1 can sugar-free green enchilada sauce
- 4 cups Monterey jack cheese
- ½ cup cilantro, chopped

Directions:
1. Put the shredded chicken in the crockpot.
2. Sour cream and enchilada sauce should be added.
3. Add Monterey Jack cheese on top.
4. Cook for 8 hours on low or 6 hours on high with the lid securely on.
5. Sprinkle cilantro on top an hour before the cooking process is finished.

Nutrition Info: Calories per serving: 469; Carbohydrates: 5g; Protein: 34g; Fat:29 g; Sugar:2.2 g; Sodium: 977mg; Fiber: 1g

Garlic Duck

Servings: 4
Cooking Time: 5 Hours
Ingredients:
- 1-pound duck fillet
- 1 tablespoon minced garlic
- 1 tablespoon butter, softened
- 1 teaspoon dried thyme
- 1/3 cup coconut cream

Directions:
1. Combine butter, dried thyme, and minced garlic.
2. After that, coat the sucker fillet with the garlic mixture and put it in the slow cooker.

3. Cook the duck for 5 hours on high with coconut cream.
4. The cooked duck fillet is then sliced, and hot garlic coconut milk is added.

Nutrition Info: Per Serving: 216 calories, 34.1g protein, 2g carbohydrates, 8.4g fat, 0.6g fiber, 8mg cholesterol, 194mg sodium, 135mg potassium.

Lemon Garlic Dump Chicken

Servings: 6
Cooking Time: 8 Hours
Ingredients:
- ¼ cup olive oil
- 2 teaspoon garlic, minced
- 6 chicken breasts, bones removed
- 1 tablespoon parsley, chopped
- 2 tablespoons lemon juice, freshly squeezed

Directions:
1. In a skillet, heat the oil over medium heat.
2. Garlic is sautéed until golden brown.
3. Put the chicken breasts in the slow cooker.
4. Pour the garlic-infused oil on top.
5. Lemon juice and parsley are added. Water should be added.

6. Cook for 8 hours on low or 6 hours on high with the lid securely on.

Nutrition Info: Calories per serving: 581; Carbohydrates: 0.7g; Protein: 60.5g; Fat: 35.8g; Sugar: 0g; Sodium: 583mg; Fiber: 0.3g

Chicken Pate

Servings: 6
Cooking Time: 8 Hours
Ingredients:
- 1 carrot, peeled
- 1 teaspoon salt
- 1-pound chicken liver
- 2 cups of water
- 2 tablespoons coconut oil

Directions:
1. The carrots should be roughly chopped and added to the crock pot.
2. Add water and chicken livers.
3. Cook the mixture on low for 8 hours.
4. After that, pour the water off and put the mixture in the blender.
5. Add salt and coconut oil.
6. Blend the mixture thoroughly.
7. For up to seven days, keep the pate in the refrigerator.

Nutrition Info: Per Serving: 169 calories, 18.6g protein, 1.7g carbohydrates, 9.5g fat, 0.3g fiber,

426mg cholesterol, 454mg sodium, 232mg potassium.

Buffalo Chicken Tenders

Servings: 4
Cooking Time: 3.5 Hours
Ingredients:
- 12 oz chicken fillet
- 3 tablespoons buffalo sauce
- ½ cup of coconut milk
- 1 jalapeno pepper, chopped

Directions:
1. Buffalo sauce is sprinkled over the chicken fillet that has been cut into tenders.
2. In the Crock-Pot, place the chicken tenders.
3. Coconut milk and jalapenos should be added.
4. Cook the food for 3.5 hours on high with the lid closed.

Nutrition Info: Per Serving: 235 calories, 25.3g protein, 2.4g carbohydrates, 13.5g fat, 1g fiber, 76mg cholesterol, 318mg sodium, 293mg potassium.

Horseradish Chicken Wings

Servings: 4
Cooking Time: 6 Hours
Ingredients:
- 3 tablespoons horseradish, grated
- 1 teaspoon ketchup
- 1 tablespoon mayonnaise
- ½ cup of water
- 1-pound chicken wings

Directions:
1. Combine ketchup, horseradish, and mayonnaise with chicken wings.
2. Add water to the crock pot and place them inside.
3. For six hours, cook the food on low.

Nutrition Info: Per Serving: 236 calories, 33g protein, 2.5g carbohydrates, 9.7g fat, 0.4g fiber, 102mg cholesterol, 174mg sodium, 309mg potassium.

Italian Style Tenders

Servings: 4
Cooking Time: 3 Hours
Ingredients:
- 12 oz chicken fillet
- 1 tablespoon Italian seasonings
- ½ cup of water
- 1 tablespoon olive oil
- 1 teaspoon salt

Directions:
1. Chicken tenders should be cut into pieces and seasoned with salt and Italian seasoning.
2. The skillet's oil is then heated.
3. Add the chicken tenders and cook them for one minute on each side over high heat.

4. Place the chicken tenders in the crock pot after that.
5. Close the cover after adding water.
6. On high, cook the chicken for three hours.

Nutrition Info: Per Serving: 202 calories, 24.6g protein, 0.4g carbohydrates, 10.8g fat, 0g fiber, 75mg cholesterol, 657mg sodium, 209mg potassium.

Chicken Florentine

Servings: 4
Cooking Time: 8 Hours
Ingredients:
- 4 chicken breasts, bones and skin removed
- Salt and pepper to taste
- 2 cups parmesan cheese, divided
- ½ cup heavy cream
- 1 cup baby spinach, rinsed

Directions:
1. Put the chicken in the slow cooker. To taste, add salt and pepper to the food.
2. Add half of the parmesan cheese and stir.
3. Cook for 8 hours on low or 6 hours on high with the lid securely on.
4. Pour the heavy cream in at the halfway point of the cooking process.

5. Cooking should go on.
6. Add the baby spinach an hour after the cooking is finished. Cook the spinach until it wilts.

Nutrition Info: Calories per serving: 553; Carbohydrates: 3g; Protein: 48g; Fat: 32g; Sugar:0 g; Sodium: 952mg; Fiber: 2.6g

Cinnamon Turkey

Servings: 5
Cooking Time: 6 Hours
Ingredients:
- 1 teaspoon ground cinnamon
- 1-pound turkey fillet, chopped
- ½ teaspoon dried thyme
- 1 teaspoon salt
- ½ cup cream

Directions:
1. Combine salt, thyme, and cinnamon with the turkey.
2. Place it in the slow cooker.
3. Cook the food on low for 6 hours after adding cream.

Nutrition Info: Per Serving: 102 calories, 19g protein, 1.1g carbohydrates, 1.8g fat, 0.2g fiber, 52mg cholesterol, 678mg sodium, 11mg potassium.

Basic Shredded Chicken

Servings: 12
Cooking Time: 8 Hours

Ingredients:

- 6 pounds chicken breasts, bones and skin removed
- 1 teaspoon salt
- ½ teaspoon black pepper
- 5 cups homemade chicken broth
- 4 tablespoons butter

Directions:

1. All ingredients should be put in the crockpot.
2. Cook for 6 hours on high or 8 hours on low while covering the pan.
3. Use two forks to shred the chicken.
4. Go back to the CrockPot and cook for an additional 30 minutes on high.

Nutrition Info: Calories per serving: 421; Carbohydrates: 0.5g; Protein: 48.1g; Fat: 25.4g; Sugar: 0g; Sodium: 802mg; Fiber: 0.1g

Rosemary Chicken In Yogurt

Servings: 4
Cooking Time: 6 Hours
Ingredients:

- 1 cup plain yogurt
- 1 tablespoon dried rosemary
- 2 tablespoons olive oil
- 1 teaspoon onion powder
- 1-pound chicken breast, skinless, boneless, chopped

Directions:

1. Olive oil, dried rosemary, and onion powder should be applied to the chicken breast.
2. Place the chicken in the slow cooker.
3. Add plain yogurt, then cover the container.
4. For six hours, cook the chicken on low.
5. Transfer the cooked food to the plates, then drizzle the plates with the hot yogurt mixture.

Nutrition Info: Per Serving: 238 calories, 27.6g protein, 5.3g carbohydrates, 10.7g fat, 0.4g fiber, 76mg cholesterol, 101mg sodium, 577mg potassium.

Ground Turkey Bowl

Servings: 4
Cooking Time: 2.5 Hours
Ingredients:

- 2 tomatoes, chopped
- 10 oz ground turkey
- 1 cup Monterey Jack cheese, shredded
- ½ cup cream
- 1 teaspoon ground black pepper

Directions:

1. In the crock pot, place the ground turkey.
2. Pepper powder, cheese, and cream should all be added.

3. Cook the food for 2.5 hours on high with the lid closed.
4. After carefully combining the ingredients, transfer the mixture to serving bowls.
5. Tomato slices are added on top of the ground turkey.

Nutrition Info: Per Serving: 275 calories, 27.2g protein, 3.9g carbohydrates, 18.1g fat, 0.9g fiber, 103mg cholesterol, 240mg sodium, 378mg potassium.

Wine Chicken

Servings: 4
Cooking Time: 3 Hours
Ingredients:
- 1 cup red wine
- 1-pound chicken breast, skinless, boneless, chopped
- 1 anise star
- 1 teaspoon cayenne pepper
- 2 garlic cloves, crushed

Directions:
1. Put some red wine in the slow cooker.
2. Add the garlic cloves, cayenne pepper, and anise seed.
3. Close the lid after adding the chopped chicken.
4. For three hours, cook the food on high.
5. Hot wine sauce should be served with the chicken.

Nutrition Info: Per Serving: 182 calories, 24.2g protein, 2.4g carbohydrates, 2.9g fat, 0.2g fiber, 73mg cholesterol, 61mg sodium, 493mg potassium.

Chicken With Green Onion Sauce

Servings: 4
Cooking Time: 4 Hrs
Ingredients:
- 2 tbsp butter, melted
- 4 green onions, chopped
- 4 chicken breast halves, skinless and boneless
- Salt and black pepper to the taste
- 8 oz. sour cream

Directions:
1. Add the chicken, remaining ingredients, and melted butter to the crock pot.
2. Put the lid on the cooker and select the high cooking setting for 4 hours.
3. Serve hot.

Nutrition Info: Per Serving: Calories: 200, Total Fat: 7g, Fiber: 2g, Total Carbs: 11g, Protein: 20g

Easy Chicken Continental

Servings: 2
Cooking Time: 7 Hours
Ingredients:
- 2 oz dried beef

- 8 oz chicken breast, skinless, boneless, chopped
- ½ cup cream
- ½ can onion soup
- 1 tablespoon cornstarch

Directions:
1. One ounce of the dried beef should be layered in the crock pot.
2. Add the remaining dried beef on top, followed by the chicken breast.
3. After that, mix cream cheese, onion, and cornstarch. Pour the mixture over the chicken and dried beef after whisking it.
4. For seven hours, cook the food on low.

Nutrition Info: Per Serving: 270 calories, 35.4g protein, 10.5g carbohydrates, 9g fat, 0.6g fiber, 109mg cholesterol, 737mg sodium, 598mg potassium.

Greece Style Chicken

Servings: 6
Cooking Time: 8 Hours
Ingredients:
- 12 oz chicken fillet, chopped
- 1 cup green olives, chopped
- 1 cup of water
- 1 tablespoon cream cheese
- ½ teaspoon dried thyme

Directions:

1. Place each ingredient in the slow cooker.
2. Cook the food on low for 8 hours with the lid shut.
3. After that, place the cooked chicken in the bowls and top with hot
4. Crock Pot liquid and olives.

Nutrition Info: Per Serving: 124 calories,16.7g protein, 0.8g carbohydrates, 5.7g fat, 0.3g fiber, 52mg cholesterol, 167mg sodium, 142mg potassium.

Chicken Sausages In Jam

Servings: 4
Cooking Time: 6 Hours
Ingredients:
- ½ cup of strawberry jam
- ½ cup of water
- 1-pound chicken breast, skinless, boneless, chopped
- 1 teaspoon white pepper

Directions:

1. Add white pepper to the chicken meat before placing it in the slow cooker.
2. After that, combine jam and water, then pour the mixture over the chicken.
3. Cook it on low for 6 hours with the lid shut.

Nutrition Info: Per Serving: 282 calories, 24.1g protein, 37.5g carbohydrates, 2.9g fat, 0.1g fiber,

73mg cholesterol, 59mg sodium, 427mg potassium.

Garlic Pulled Chicken

Servings: 4
Cooking Time: 4 Hours
Ingredients:

- 1-pound chicken breast, skinless, boneless
- 1 tablespoon minced garlic
- 2 cups of water
- ½ cup plain yogurt

Directions:

1. In the Crock-Pot, place the chicken breasts.
2. Add water and minced garlic.
3. Cook the chicken for 4 hours on high with the lid securely on.
4. Drain the water after that, and shred the chicken breast.
5. Stir in plain yogurt after adding it to the pulled chicken.

Nutrition Info: Per Serving: 154 calories, 25.9g protein, 2.9g carbohydrates, 3.2g fat, 0g fiber, 74mg cholesterol, 83mg sodium, 501mg potassium.

Vinegar Chicken Wings

Servings: 8
Cooking Time: 3 Hours
Ingredients:

- ½ cup apple cider vinegar
- 1 teaspoon garlic powder
- 1 teaspoon smoked paprika
- ½ cup plain yogurt
- 3-pounds chicken wings

Directions:

1. Combine plain yogurt with apple cider vinegar, smoked paprika, and garlic powder.
2. Fill the crock pot with the liquid.
3. Add the chicken wings, then cover the pan.
4. For three hours, cook the food on high.

Nutrition Info: Per Serving: 339 calories, 50.2g protein, 1.6g carbohydrates, 12.8g fat, 0.1g fiber, 152mg cholesterol, 158mg sodium, 470mg potassium.

Lemon Parsley Chicken

Servings: 4
Cooking Time: 8 Hours
Ingredients:

- 2 tablespoons butter, melted
- 1-pound chicken breasts, bones removed
- Salt and pepper to taste
- 1 lemon, sliced thinly
- ½ cup parsley, chopped

Directions:

1. Foil should be used to line the crockpot's bottom.
2. To grease the foil, melt some butter.
3. Add salt and pepper to taste and season the chicken breasts.

4. Place the arrangement on the foil, then add the lemon slices.
5. Add some chopped parsley.
6. Cook for eight hours on low or six hours on high.

Nutrition Info: Calories per serving: 303; Carbohydrates: 3.1g; Protein: 34.5g; Fat: 14g; Sugar: 0.7g; Sodium: 430mg; Fiber: 1g

Fish & Seafood Recipes

Curry Shrimps

Servings: 4
Cooking Time: 45 Minutes
Ingredients:

- 16 oz shrimps, peeled
- 1 teaspoon curry paste
- ½ cup fish stock

Directions:

1. Pour in the crock pot after combining the curry paste and fish stock.
2. Add the shrimp and cook them for 45 minutes on high.

Nutrition Info: Per Serving: 148 calories, 26.6g protein, 2.1g carbohydrates, 2.9g fat, 0g fiber, 239mg cholesterol, 322mg sodium, 234mg potassium

Smelt In Avocado Oil

Servings: 4
Cooking Time: 4 Hours
Ingredients:

- 12 oz smelt fillet
- 1 teaspoon chili powder
- ¼ teaspoon ground turmeric
- ½ teaspoon smoked paprika
- 4 tablespoons avocado oil

Directions:

1. The smelt fillet should serve 4 people.
2. Then add smoked paprika, ground turmeric, and chili powder to each fish fillet.
3. Place the fish in the slow cooker.
4. Place the lid on after adding avocado oil.
5. For four hours, cook the fish on low.

Nutrition Info: Per Serving: 89 calories, 13.1g protein, 1.4g carbohydrates, 3.5g fat, 1g fiber, 112mg cholesterol, 52mg sodium, 66mg potassium

Curry Clams

Servings: 4
Cooking Time: 1.5 Hour
Ingredients:

- 1-pound clams
- 1 teaspoon curry paste
- ¼ cup of coconut milk
- 1 cup of water

Directions:

1. Pour the coconut milk, curry paste, and water into the crock pot.
2. Add the clams, then cover the pot.
3. Until the clams open, cook the dish on high for 1.5 hours.

Nutrition Info: Per Serving: 97 calories, 1.1g protein, 13.6g

carbohydrates, 4.5g fat, 0.8g fiber, 0mg cholesterol, 415mg sodium, 141mg potassium.

Turmeric Mackerel

Servings: 4
Cooking Time: 2.5 Hours
Ingredients:
- 1-pound mackerel fillet
- 1 tablespoon ground turmeric
- ½ teaspoon salt
- ¼ teaspoon chili powder
- ½ cup of water

Directions:
1. Sprinkle ground turmeric and chili powder on the mackerel fillet.
2. Put it in the crock pot after that.
3. Add salt and water.
4. Fish should be cooked for 2.5 hours on high with the lid closed.

Nutrition Info: Per Serving: 304 calories, 27.2g protein, 1.2g carbohydrates, 20.4g fat, 0.4g fiber, 58mg cholesterol, 388mg sodium, 501mg potassium

Mackerel Bites

Servings: 4
Cooking Time: 3 Hours
Ingredients:
- 1-pound mackerel fillet, chopped
- 1 tablespoon avocado oil
- ½ teaspoon ground paprika
- ½ teaspoon ground turmeric
- 1/3 cup water

Directions:
1. Combine ground turmeric and ground paprika in a small bowl.
2. The spice mixture should then be sprinkled over the mackerel fillet.
3. In the skillet, thoroughly warm the avocado oil.
4. On high heat, add the fish and roast it for one minute on each side.
5. Fill up the crock pot with water.
6. After adding the fish, cover the pot.
7. On high, prepare the mackerel bites for three hours.

Nutrition Info: Per Serving: 304 calories, 27.2g protein, 0.5g carbohydrates, 20.7g fat, 0.3g fiber, 85mg cholesterol, 95mg sodium, 479mg potassium

Basil Octopus

Servings: 3
Cooking Time: 4 Hours
Ingredients:
- 12 oz octopus, chopped
- 1 orange, chopped

- 1 teaspoon dried basil
- ½ cup of water
- 1 teaspoon butter

Directions:

1. Place each item in the slow cooker.
2. The octopus should be cooked on low for 4 hours or until it is tender. Close the lid.

Nutrition Info: Per Serving: 226 calories, 34.4g protein, 12.2g carbohydrates, 3.7g fat, 1.5g fiber, 112mg cholesterol, 532mg sodium, 827mg potassium

Lemony Shrimps In Hoisin Sauce

Servings: 4
Cooking Time: 2 Hours
Ingredients:

- 1/3 cup hoisin sauce
- ½ cup lemon juice, freshly squeezed
- 1 ½ pounds shrimps, shelled and deveined
- Salt and pepper to taste
- 2 tablespoon cilantro leaves, chopped

Directions:

1. The hoisin sauce, lemon juice, and shrimp are added to the slow cooker.
2. To taste, add salt and pepper to the food.

The ingredients should all be combined.

3. Put the lid on and cook for 30 minutes on high or two hours on low.
4. Add cilantro leaves as a garnish.

Nutrition Info: Calories per serving: 228; Carbohydrates: 6.3g; Protein: 35.8g; Fat: 3.2g; Sugar: 0g; Sodium: 482mg; Fiber: 4.8g

Mustard Cod

Servings: 4
Cooking Time: 3 Hours
Ingredients:

- 4 cod fillets
- 4 teaspoons mustard
- 2 tablespoons sesame oil
- ¼ cup of water

Directions:

1. Combine sesame oil and mustard.
2. After that, place the cod fillets in the crockpot and brush with the mustard mixture.
3. Cook the fish on low for three hours while adding water.

Nutrition Info: Per Serving: 166 calories, 20.8g protein, 1.2g carbohydrates, 8.8g fat, 0.5g fiber, 55mg cholesterol, 71mg sodium, 23mg potassium

Prosciutto-wrapped Scallops

Servings: 4
Cooking Time: 3 Hours
Ingredients:
- 12 large scallops, rinsed and patted dry
- Salt and pepper to taste
- 1 ¼ ounces prosciutto, cut into 12 long strips
- 1 tablespoon extra-virgin olive oil
- 1 tablespoon lemon juice

Directions:
1. To taste, season each scallop with salt and pepper.
2. Scallops should be surrounded by prosciutto. Place aside.
3. The scallops wrapped in bacon are placed on top of the oil-filled crockpot.
4. The lemon juice on top.
5. Cook for one hour on low or three hours on high.
6. Flip the scallops halfway through the cooking process.
7. Cook the scallops for a while longer.

Nutrition Info: Calories per serving: 113; Carbohydrates: 5g; Protein: 15.9g; Fat:8 g; Sugar:0 g; Sodium: 424mg; Fiber: 3.2g

Vegan Milk Clams

Servings: 4
Cooking Time: 3 Hours
Ingredients:
- 1 cup organic almond milk
- 1 teaspoon dried parsley
- 1 teaspoon dried dill
- ½ teaspoon salt
- 1-pound clams

Directions:
1. Mix gently after adding all the ingredients to the crock pot. Clams should be cooked on low for three hours with the lid on.

Nutrition Info: Per Serving: 70 calories, 1g protein, 14.6g carbohydrates, 0.9g fat, 0.5g fiber, 0mg cholesterol, 737mg sodium, 111mg potassium

Sweet And Sour Shrimps

Servings: 2
Cooking Time: 50 Minutes
Ingredients:
- 8 oz shrimps, peeled
- ½ cup of water
- 2 tablespoons lemon juice
- 1 tablespoon maple syrup

Directions:
1. Fill up the crock pot with water.
2. Add the shrimp and cook them for 50 minutes on high.
3. Drain the water and add maple syrup and lemon juice.
4. Stir the shrimps gently, then place them in the serving bowls.

Nutrition Info: Per Serving: 165 calories, 26g protein, 8.8g carbohydrates, 2.1g fat, 0.1g fiber, 239mg cholesterol, 282mg sodium, 232mg potassium.

Braised Salmon

Servings: 4
Cooking Time: 1 Hour
Ingredients:
- 1 cup of water
- 2-pound salmon fillet
- 1 teaspoon salt
- 1 teaspoon ground black pepper

Directions:
1. Close the lid on the Crock Pot after adding all the ingredients. Cook the salmon on high for 1 hour.

Nutrition Info: Per Serving: 301 calories, 44.1g protein, 0.3g carbohydrates, 14g fat, 0.1g fiber, 100mg cholesterol, 683mg sodium, 878mg potassium.

Apple Cider Vinegar Sardines

Servings: 4
Cooking Time: 4.5 Hours
Ingredients:
- 14 oz sardines
- 1 tablespoon butter
- ¼ cup apple cider vinegar
- ½ teaspoon cayenne pepper

- 4 tablespoons coconut cream

Directions:
1. Place the sardines in the slow cooker.
2. Add coconut cream, butter, apple cider vinegar, and cayenne pepper.
3. Cook the food on low for 4.5 hours with the lid shut.

Nutrition Info: Per Serving: 270 calories, 24.8g protein, 1.1g carbohydrates, 17.9g fat, 0.4g fiber, 149mg cholesterol,525mg sodium, 450mg potassium

Buttered Bacon And Scallops

Servings: 4
Cooking Time: 2 Hours
Ingredients:
- 1 tablespoon butter
- 2 cloves of garlic, chopped
- 24 scallops, rinsed and patted dry
- Salt and pepper to taste
- 1 cup bacon, chopped

Directions:
1. Butter should be heated in a skillet while the garlic is sautéed until fragrant and lightly browned.
2. Add the scallops and move to a crockpot.
3. To taste, add salt and pepper to the food.

4. Cook for 45 minutes on high or two hours on low with the lid closed.
5. During this time, cook the bacon until the fat has rendered and it is crispy.
6. Crispy bacon should be added to the cooked scallops.

Nutrition Info: Calories per serving: 261; Carbohydrates:4.9 g; Protein:24.7 g; Fat:14.3 g; Sugar: 1.3g; Sodium: 425mg; Fiber: 3g

Almond-crusted Tilapia

Servings: 4
Cooking Time: 4 Hours
Ingredients:
- 2 tablespoons olive oil
- 1 cup chopped almonds
- ¼ cup ground flaxseed
- 4 tilapia fillets
- Salt and pepper to taste

Directions:
1. Foil should be used to line the crockpot's bottom.
2. Use the olive oil to grease the foil.
3. Almonds and flaxseed should be combined in a mixing bowl.
4. Add salt and pepper to taste when preparing the tilapia.
5. Tilapia fillets should be dredged in the almond and flaxseed mixture.

6. Place the chicken in the crockpot lined with foil in an orderly fashion.
7. Cook for 2 hours on high and 4 hours on low while covering the pan.

Nutrition Info: Calories per serving: 233; Carbohydrates: 4.6g; Protein: 25.5g; Fat: 13.3g; Sugar: 0.4g; Sodium: 342mg; Fiber: 1.9g

Salmon With Green Peppercorn Sauce

Servings: 4
Cooking Time: 3 Hours
Ingredients:
- 1 ¼ pounds salmon fillets, skin removed and cut into 4 portions
- Salt and pepper to taste
- 4 teaspoons unsalted butter
- ¼ cup lemon juice
- 1 teaspoon green peppercorns in vinegar

Directions:
1. To taste, season the salmon fillets with salt and pepper.
2. Butter should be heated in a skillet before searing the salmon fillets for two minutes on each side.
3. Add the green peppercorns and lemon juice after transferring to the slow cooker.

4. Depending on your preference, add more salt or pepper to the dish to adjust the seasoning.
5. Cook for one hour on high or three hours on low while covering the pan.

Nutrition Info: Calories per serving: 255; Carbohydrates: 2.3g; Protein: 37.4g; Fat: 13.5g; Sugar: 0g; Sodium: 352mg; Fiber: 1.5g

Salmon Stew

Servings: 6
Cooking Time: 5 Hours 15 Minutes
Ingredients:
- 2 tablespoons butter
- 2 pounds salmon fillet, cubed
- 2 medium onions, chopped
- Salt and black pepper, to taste
- 2 cups homemade fish broth

Directions:
1. Mix each ingredient well before adding it to the one-pot crock pot.
2. For about 5 hours on LOW, cook covered.
3. After dishing it out, serve it hot.

Nutrition Info: Calories: 293 Fat: 8.7g Carbohydrates: 16.3g

Thyme And Sesame Halibut

Servings: 2
Cooking Time: 4 Hours
Ingredients:
- 1 tablespoon lemon juice
- 1 teaspoon thyme
- Salt and pepper to taste
- 8 ounces halibut or mahi-mahi, cut into 2 portions
- 1 tablespoons sesame seeds, toasted

Directions:
1. Foil should be used to line the crockpot's bottom.
2. In a shallow dish, combine salt, pepper, lemon juice, and thyme.
3. Place the fish there and give it two hours to marinate.
4. Add some toasted sesame seeds to the fish.
5. Put the fish in the crockpot that is lined with foil.
6. Cook for 2 hours on high or 4 hours on low while covering the pan.

Nutrition Info: Calories per serving: 238; Carbohydrates: 3.9g; Protein: 23.1g; Fat: 14.9g; Sugar: 0.5g; Sodium:313 mg; Fiber:1.6 g

Miso Cod

Servings: 4
Cooking Time: 4 Hours

Ingredients:

- 1-pound cod fillet, sliced
- 1 teaspoon miso paste
- ½ teaspoon ground ginger
- 2 cups chicken stock
- ½ teaspoon ground nutmeg

Directions:

1. Combine chicken stock, miso paste, ground ginger, and nutmeg in a mixing bowl.
2. Then fill the crock pot with the liquid.
3. Seal the lid after adding the cod fillet.
4. For four hours, cook the salmon on low.

Nutrition Info: Per Serving: 101 calories, 20.8g protein, 1.1g carbohydrates, 1.5g fat, 0.2g fiber, 56mg cholesterol, 506mg sodium, 14mg potassium.

Butter Crab Legs

Servings: 4
Cooking Time: 45 Minutes
Ingredients:

- 15 oz king crab legs
- 1 tablespoon butter
- 1 cup of water
- 1 teaspoon dried basil

Directions:

1. In the crock pot, place the crab legs.
2. Cook for 45 minutes on high with basil and water.

Nutrition Info: Per Serving: 133 calories, 20.4g protein, 0g carbohydrates, 4.5g fat, 0g fiber, 67mg cholesterol, 1161mg sodium, 2mg potassium

Bigeye Jack Saute

Servings: 4
Cooking Time: 6 Hours
Ingredients:

- 7 oz (bigeye jack) tuna fillet, chopped
- 1 cup tomato, chopped
- 1 teaspoon ground black pepper
- 1 jalapeno pepper, chopped
- ½ cup chicken stock

Directions:

1. Close the lid on the Crock Pot after adding all the ingredients. For six hours, cook the saute on low.

Nutrition Info: Per Serving: 192 calories, 11g protein, 2.4g carbohydrates, 15.6g fat, 0.8g fiber, 0mg cholesterol, 98mg sodium, 123mg potassium

Spicy Basil Shrimp

Servings: 4
Cooking Time: 2 Hours
Ingredients:

- 1-pound raw shrimp, shelled and deveined
- Salt and pepper to taste

- 1 tablespoon butter
- ¼ cup packed fresh basil leaves
- ¼ teaspoon cayenne pepper

Directions:
1. Place each ingredient in the slow cooker.
2. Create a stir.
3. Put the lid on and cook for 30 minutes on high or two hours on low.

Nutrition Info: Calories per serving: 144; Carbohydrates: 1.4g; Protein: 23.4g; Fat: 6.2g; Sugar: 0g; Sodium: 126mg; Fiber:0.5 g

Parsley Salmon

Servings: 6
Cooking Time: 5 Hours 30 Minutes
Ingredients:
- ¼ teaspoon ginger powder
- 2 tablespoons olive oil
- 24-ounce salmon fillets
- Salt and black pepper, to taste
- 3 tablespoons fresh parsley, minced

Directions:
1. In a bowl, combine all the ingredients with the exception of the salmon fillets.

2. Salmon fillets should be marinated in this mixture for about an hour.
3. Place the salmon fillets that have been marinated in the crock pot and secure the lid.
4. Cook for approximately 5 hours on low, then dish out to serve hot.

Nutrition Info: Calories: 191 Fat: 11.7 g Carbohydrates: 0.2 g

Taco Mackerel

Servings: 4
Cooking Time: 1.5 Hours
Ingredients:
- 12 oz mackerel fillets
- 1 tablespoon taco seasonings
- 2 tablespoons coconut oil
- 3 tablespoons water

Directions:
1. Warm the skillet while melting the coconut oil.
2. Rub the taco seasonings into the mackerel fillets while you wait.
3. In the hot coconut oil, place the fish.
4. For two minutes on each side, roast it.
5. Afterward, put the roasted fish in the slow cooker.
6. Cook it for 1.5 hours on high after adding water.

Nutrition Info: Per Serving: 289 calories, 20.3g protein, 1g carbohydrates, 22g fat, 0g fiber, 64mg cholesterol, 176mg sodium, 341mg potassium

Scallops With Sour Cream And Dill

Servings: 4
Cooking Time: 2 Hours
Ingredients:
- 1 ¼ pounds scallops
- Salt and pepper to taste
- 3 teaspoons butter
- ¼ cup sour cream
- 1 tablespoon fresh dill

Directions:
1. Place each item in the slow cooker.
2. To thoroughly incorporate everything, whisk it well.
3. Put the cover on and cook for 30 minutes on high or two hours on low.

Nutrition Info: Calories per serving: 152; Carbohydrates: 4.3g; Protein: 18.2g; Fat: 5.7g; Sugar: 0.5g; Sodium: 231mg; Fiber: 2.3g

Butter Tilapia

Servings: 4
Cooking Time: 6 Hours
Ingredients:
- 4 tilapia fillets

- ½ cup butter
- 1 teaspoon dried dill
- ½ teaspoon ground black pepper

Directions:
1. Add ground black pepper and dried dill to the tilapia fillets. Put them in the slow cooker.
2. Put butter in.
   Tilapia should be cooked on low for 6 hours.

Nutrition Info: Per Serving: 298 calories, 21.3g protein, 0.3g carbohydrates, 24.1g fat, 0.1g fiber, 116mg cholesterol, 204mg sodium, 18mg potassium

Crab Bake

Servings: 4
Cooking Time: 1.5 Hours
Ingredients:
- 1 cup Cheddar cheese, shredded
- 1-pound crab meat, cooked, chopped
- 1 teaspoon white pepper
- 1 teaspoon dried cilantro
- 1 cup cream

Directions:
1. Lay the crab meat out in a single layer in the Crock Pot.
2. Add some dried cilantro and white pepper to it.

3. Pour the cream after that, and top the crab meat with Cheddar cheese.

Nutrition Info: Per Serving: 255 calories, 21.8g protein, 4.6g carbohydrates, 14.7g fat, 0.1g fiber, 102mg cholesterol, 904mg sodium, 57mg potassium.

Garlic Perch

Servings: 4
Cooking Time: 4 Hours
Ingredients:
- 1-pound perch
- 1 teaspoon minced garlic
- 1 tablespoon butter, softened
- 1 tablespoon fish sauce
- ½ cup of water

Directions:
1. Mix the fish sauce, butter, and minced garlic in a shallow bowl.
2. After brushing the perch with the garlic butter mixture, place it in the crock pot.
3. Pour in the remaining garlic butter mixture and water.
4. For four hours, cook the fish on high.

Nutrition Info: Per Serving: 161 calories, 28.5g protein, 0.4g carbohydrates, 4.2g fat, 0g fiber, 138mg cholesterol, 458mg sodium, 407mg potassium.

Soy Sauce Scallops

Servings: 4
Cooking Time: 30 Minutes
Ingredients:
- ¼ cup of soy sauce
- 1 tablespoon butter
- ½ teaspoon white pepper
- 1-pound scallops

Directions:
1. Put some soy sauce in the slow cooker.
2. Add white pepper and butter.
3. Add scallops next, then cover the pan.
4. For thirty minutes, cook them on high.

Nutrition Info: Per Serving: 134 calories, 20.1g protein, 4.1g carbohydrates, 3.8g fat, 0.2g fiber, 45mg cholesterol, 1102mg sodium, 404mg potassium

Cod With Asparagus

Servings: 4
Cooking Time: 2 Hrs
Ingredients:
- 4 cod fillets, boneless
- 1 bunch asparagus
- 12 tbsp lemon juice
- Salt and black pepper to the taste
- 2 tbsp olive oil

Directions:
1. Cod fillets should be placed on separate foil sheets.

2. Asparagus spears, lemon pepper, oil, and lemon juice are sprinkled on top of the fish.
3. Place the fish in the crock pot after wrapping it in foil.
4. Put the cover on the cooker and choose a high cooking mode for 2 hours.
5. Serve the fish warm after unwrapping it.

Nutrition Info: Per Serving: Calories 202, Total Fat 3g, Fiber 6g, Total Carbs 7g, Protein 3g

Coconut Curry Cod

Servings: 2
Cooking Time: 2.5 Hours
Ingredients:
- 2 cod fillets
- ½ teaspoon curry paste
- 1/3 cup coconut milk
- 1 teaspoon sunflower oil

Directions:
1. Combine coconut milk and curry paste, add sunflower oil, and pour the mixture into a slow cooker.
2. Put in cod fillets.
3. Cook the food for 2.5 hours on high.

Nutrition Info: Per Serving: 211 calories, 21g protein, 2.6g carbohydrates, 13.6g fat, 0.9g fiber, 55mg cholesterol, 76mg sodium, 105mg potassium

Cilantro Haddock

Servings: 2
Cooking Time: 1.5 Hour
Ingredients:
- 6 oz haddock fillet
- 1 teaspoon dried cilantro
- 1 teaspoon olive oil
- 1 teaspoon lemon juice
- ¼ cup fish stock

Directions:
1. The skillet's olive oil is nicely warmed.
2. The haddock fillet is then placed on the grill and roasted for one minute on each side.
3. Place the fillets in the slow cooker.
4. Add fish stock, lemon juice, and cilantro.
5. Fish needs 1.5 hours on high to cook.

Nutrition Info: Per Serving: 121 calories, 21.3g protein, 0.1g carbohydrates, 3.4g fat, 0g fiber, 63mg cholesterol, 120mg sodium, 385mg potassium

Soy Sauce Catfish

Servings: 4
Cooking Time: 5 Hours
Ingredients:
- 1-pound catfish fillet, chopped
- ¼ cup of soy sauce
- 1 jalapeno pepper, diced

- 1 tablespoon olive oil
- 4 tablespoons fish stock

Directions:

1. Add some olive oil to the catfish before placing it in the slow cooker.
2. Add the fish stock, jalapeno pepper, and soy sauce.
3. Cook the food on low for 5 hours with the lid securely on.

Nutrition Info: Per Serving: 195 calories, 19g protein, 1.4g carbohydrates, 12.3g fat, 0.2g fiber, 53mg cholesterol, 981mg sodium, 427mg potassium

Sweet Milkfish Saute

Servings: 4
Cooking Time: 3 Hours
Ingredients:

- 2 mangos, pitted, peeled, chopped
- 12 oz milkfish fillet, chopped
- ½ cup tomatoes, chopped
- ½ cup of water
- 1 teaspoon ground cardamom

Directions:

1. Combine mangos, tomatoes, and cardamom powder.
2. Fill the crock pot with the ingredients.
3. Add water and milkfish fillet after that.

4. For three hours on high, cook the sauté.
5. Before serving, give the saute a gentle stir.

Nutrition Info: Per Serving: 268 calories, 24g protein, 26.4g carbohydrates, 8.1g fat, 3.1g fiber, 57mg cholesterol, 82mg sodium, 660mg potassium.

Miso-poached Cod

Servings: 4
Cooking Time: 2.5 Hours
Ingredients:

- 1 teaspoon miso paste
- ½ cup of water
- ½ teaspoon dried lemongrass
- 4 cod fillets
- 1 teaspoon olive oil

Directions:

1. Olive oil, dried lemongrass, and miso paste should be combined.
2. Then fill the crock pot with the liquid.
3. Put in cod fillets.
4. Cook the cod for 2.5 hours on high.

Nutrition Info: Per Serving: 103 calories, 20.2g protein, 0.4g carbohydrates, 2.3g fat, 0.1g fiber, 55mg cholesterol, 124mg sodium, 5mg potassium

Salmon With Lime Butter

Servings: 4

Cooking Time: 4 Hours

Ingredients:

- 1-pound salmon fillet cut into 4 portions
- 1 tablespoon butter, melted
- Salt and pepper to taste
- 2 tablespoons lime juice
- ½ teaspoon lime zest, grated

Directions:

1. Place each item in the slow cooker.
   Put the lid on.
   Cook for 2 hours on high and 4 hours on low.

Nutrition Info: Calories per serving: 206; Carbohydrates: 1.8g; Protein:23.7 g; Fat: 15.2g; Sugar: 0g; Sodium:235 mg; Fiber: 0.5g

Lunch & Dinner Recipes

Pesto Freekeh

Servings: 4
Cooking Time: 2 Hours
Ingredients:
- 2 tablespoons pesto sauce
- 1 tablespoon sesame oil
- 1 oz raisins
- 1 cup freekeh
- 3 cups chicken stock

Directions:
1. Fill the crock pot with the chicken stock.
2. Cook the ingredients for 2 hours on high with the addition of freekeh and raisins. The freekeh should be soft after cooking.
3. Then fill the basin halfway with the freekeh mixture.
4. Add pesto sauce and sesame oil.
5. Mix the food well.

Nutrition Info: Per Serving: 125 calories, 3.5g protein, 13.2g carbohydrates, 7.4g fat, 1.4g fiber, 2mg cholesterol, 621mg sodium, 64mg potassium.

Buttered Broccoli

Servings: 4
Cooking Time: 1 1/2 Hours
Ingredients:
- 2 heads broccoli, cut into florets
- 1 shallot, sliced
- 2 garlic cloves, chopped
- 4 tablespoons butter
- Salt and pepper to taste

Directions:
1. Place each item in the crock pot.
2. Cook the broccoli on high for 1 1/4 hours, seasoning it with the appropriate amount of salt and pepper.
3. Warm and fresh broccoli should be served.

Sweet Farro

Servings: 3
Cooking Time: 6 Hours
Ingredients:
- ½ cup farro
- 2 cups of water
- ½ cup heavy cream
- 2 tablespoons dried cranberries
- 2 tablespoons sugar

Directions:
1. Place the chopped cranberries in the crock pot.
2. Farro, heavy cream, sugar, and water are added.

3. With the aid of the spoon, combine the ingredients, then cover the container.
4. Farro must be cooked on low for six hours.

Nutrition Info: Per Serving: 208 calories, 5.1g protein, 31g carbohydrates, 7.4g fat, 2.2g fiber, 27mg cholesterol, 32mg sodium, 24mg potassium.

Cauliflower Mashed Sweet Potato

Servings: 6
Cooking Time: 6 1/4 Hours
Ingredients:
- 1 head cauliflower, cut into florets
- 1 pound sweet potatoes, peeled and cubed
- 1 shallot, chopped
- 2 garlic cloves, chopped
- 1 cup vegetable stock
- Salt and pepper to taste

Directions:
1. Place each item in the crock pot.
2. After adding salt and pepper to taste, simmer on low for six hours.
3. When ready, use a potato masher to mash the mixture and serve it warm.

Cod And Asparagus

Servings: 4
Cooking Time: 2 Hours
Ingredients:
- 4 cod fillets, boneless
- 1 bunch asparagus
- 12 tablespoons lemon juice
- Salt and black pepper to the taste
- 2 tablespoons olive oil

Directions:
1. Cod fillets should be divided among pieces of tin foil, then topped with asparagus spears, lemon juice, lemon pepper, and oil before being wrapped.
2. Place the wrapped fish in the crock pot, secure the lid, and cook for two hours on high.
3. Lunch should be served with the fish and asparagus removed from their packaging.

Nutrition Info: calories 202, fat 3, fiber 6, carbs 7, protein 3

Three Pepper Roasted Pork Tenderloin

Servings: 8
Cooking Time: 8 1/4 Hours
Ingredients:
- 3 pounds pork tenderloin
- 2 tablespoons Dijon mustard
- 1/4 cup three pepper mix
- Salt and pepper to taste
- 1 cup chicken stock

Directions:

1. Put salt and pepper on the meat to season it.
2. Use mustard to coat the meat. On the cutting board, spread the pepper mixture out. Roll the pork through the mixture, being sure to thoroughly coat it.
3. Place in the crock pot with care, then add the stock.
4. 8 hours of cooking on low settings
5. Sliced and heated, serve the pork tenderloin with your preferred side dish.

Mango Chutney Pork Chops

Servings: 4
Cooking Time: 5 1/4 Hours
Ingredients:
- 4 pork chops
- 1 jar mango chutney
- 3/4 cup chicken stock
- 1 bay leaf
- Salt and pepper to taste

Directions:
1. Put every ingredient into your crock pot.
2. Cook for 5 hours on low with the appropriate amount of salt and pepper.
3. Warm pork chops are best served.

Salted Caramel Rice Pudding

Servings: 2
Cooking Time: 3 Hours
Ingredients:
- 2 teaspoons salted caramel
- ½ cup basmati rice
- cup milk
- 1 teaspoon vanilla extract

Directions:
1. Fill the crock pot with milk.
2. Add basmati rice and vanilla extract.
3. For three hours on high, cook the rice.
4. After that, carefully combine the pudding with the salted caramel.
5. Transfer it into the bowls after cooling it to room temperature.

Nutrition Info: Per Serving: 284 calories, 9.8g protein, 48.9g carbohydrates, 4.7g fat, 0.8g fiber, 16mg cholesterol, 99mg sodium, 161mg potassium.

Crock Pot Steamed Rice

Servings: 8
Cooking Time: 4 Hours
Ingredients:
- 2 cups white rice
- 4 cups water
- 1 bay leaf
- Salt and pepper to taste

Directions:
1. Put every item into your crock pot.

2. Cook for 4 hours on low heat with the appropriate amounts of salt and pepper. Whenever possible, stir once while cooking.
3. As a side dish for your preferred vegetable main dish, serve the rice warm or chilled.

Beans And Peas Bowl

Servings: 4
Cooking Time: 6 Hours
Ingredients:
- ½ cup black beans, soaked
- 1 cup green peas
- 4 cups of water
- 1 tablespoon tomato paste
- 1 teaspoon sriracha

Directions:
1. Fill up the crock pot with water.
2. Cook the black beans for 5 hours on high after adding them.
3. Then add tomato paste, sriracha, and green peas.
4. The food should be stirred and cooked for an hour on high.

Nutrition Info: Per Serving: 117 calories, 7.4g protein, 21.4g carbohydrates, 0.5g fat, 5.7g fiber, 0mg cholesterol, 23mg sodium, 491mg potassium.

Green Lentils Salad

Servings: 2
Cooking Time: 4 Hours
Ingredients:
- ¼ cup green lentils
- 1 cup chicken stock
- ½ teaspoon ground cumin
- 2 cups lettuce, chopped
- ¼ cup Greek Yogurt

Directions:
1. In the crock pot, combine green lentils and chicken stock.
2. For four hours on high, cook the ingredients.
3. The lentils are then transferred to the salad bowl to cool.
4. Add Greek yogurt, lettuce, and ground cumin.
5. Toss the salad well.

Nutrition Info: Per Serving: 118 calories, 9.4g protein, 17.7g carbohydrates, 1.3g fat, 7.7g fiber, 1mg cholesterol, 395mg sodium, 359mg potassium.

Fragrant Turmeric Beans

Servings: 4
Cooking Time: 8 Hours
Ingredients:
- 1 jalapeno pepper, sliced
- 1 oz fresh ginger, grated
- 1 teaspoon ground turmeric
- 2 cups black beans, soaked
- 5 cups chicken stock

Directions:

1. Place black beans in the slow cooker.
2. Add chicken stock, ginger, turmeric, and jalapeo pepper.
3. For eight hours, cook the food on low.

Nutrition Info: Per Serving: 371 calories, 22.5g protein, 67g carbohydrates, 2.6g fat, 15.9g fiber, 0mg cholesterol, 962mg sodium, 1573mg potassium.

Asparagus Casserole

Servings: 6
Cooking Time: 6 1/2 Hours
Ingredients:

- 1 bunch asparagus, trimmed and chopped
- 1 can condensed cream of mushroom soup
- 2 hard-boiled eggs, peeled and cubed
- 1 cup grated Cheddar
- 2 cups bread croutons
- Salt and pepper to taste

Directions:
1. In your crock pot, combine the asparagus, mushroom soup, hard-boiled eggs, cheese, and bread croutons.
2. After adding salt and pepper to taste, cook on low for six hours.
3. A warm and fresh casserole should be served.

Tomato Soy Glazed Chicken

Servings: 8
Cooking Time: 8 1/4 Hours
Ingredients:

- 8 chicken thighs
- 1/2 cup soy sauce
- 2 tablespoons brown sugar
- 1 teaspoon chili powder
- 1/2 cup tomato sauce

Directions:
1. Put every ingredient into your crock pot.
2. For eight hours, the chicken should be cooked on low.
3. Warm and fresh chicken should be served.

Cheesy Chicken

Servings: 2
Cooking Time: 2 1/4 Hours
Ingredients:

- 2 chicken breasts
- 1 cup cream of chicken soup
- 1 cup grated Cheddar
- 1/4 teaspoon garlic powder
- Salt and pepper to taste

Directions:
1. Put every ingredient into your crock pot.
   Put a lid on it after adding salt and pepper to taste.
   Cook for two hours on the highest setting.

2. Warm chicken should be served with lots of cheese sauce on top.

Apple Cups

Servings: 2
Cooking Time: 6 Hours
Ingredients:
- 2 green apples
- 3 oz white rice
- 1 shallot, diced
- ¼ cup of water
- 1 tablespoon cream cheese

Directions:
1. To make the apple cups, scoop out the apple flesh.
2. After that, combine the onion, rice, and curry paste.
3. Fill up the crock pot with water.
4. Then combine the raisins, diced onion, white rice, salt, and curry powder. Fill the apple cups with the rice mixture and top with cream cheese.
5. For six hours, cook the food on low.

Nutrition Info: Per Serving: 292 calories, 4.1g protein, 65.8g carbohydrates, 2.4g fat, 6g fiber, 6mg cholesterol, 20mg sodium, 310mg potassium.

Oregano Millet

Servings: 3
Cooking Time: 3 Hours
Ingredients:
- ¼ cup heavy cream
- ½ cup millet
- 1 teaspoon dried oregano
- 1 cup of water

Directions:
1. In the crock pot, combine all the ingredients from the above list.
2. Cook for 3 hours on high with the lid closed.

Nutrition Info: Per Serving: 162 calories, 3.9g protein, 24.9g carbohydrates, 5.2g fat, 3g fiber, 14mg cholesterol, 6mg sodium, 81mg potassium.

Milky Semolina

Servings: 2
Cooking Time: 1 Hour
Ingredients:
- ¼ cup semolina
- 1 ½ cup milk
- 1 teaspoon vanilla extract
- 1 teaspoon sugar

Directions:
1. Place each ingredient in the slow cooker.
2. Semolina should be cooked for an hour on high with the lid closed.

3. When the meal is finished cooking, give it a gentle stir and let it cool to room temperature.

Nutrition Info: Per Serving: 180 calories, 8.7g protein, 26.5g carbohydrates, 4g fat, 0.8g fiber, 15mg cholesterol, 87mg sodium, 147mg potassium.

Creamed Sweet Corn

Servings: 6
Cooking Time: 3 1/4 Hours
Ingredients:

- 2 cans (15 oz.) sweet corn, drained
- 1 cup cream cheese
- 1 cup grated Cheddar cheese
- 1/2 cup heavy cream
- Salt and pepper to taste
- 1 pinch nutmeg

Directions:

1. In your crock pot, combine the corn, cream cheese, cheddar, and milk.
2. Salt, pepper, and nutmeg should be added before cooking on low for three hours.
3. Warm creamed corn is ready to serve.

Parmesan Artichokes

Servings: 2
Cooking Time: 4 1/4 Hours
Ingredients:

- 2 large artichokes

- 1/4 cup breadcrumbs
- 1/2 cup grated Parmesan
- 1/2 cup vegetable stock

Directions:

1. The artichokes must be cut and cleaned.
2. In a bowl, combine the cheese and breadcrumbs.
3. This mixture should be placed on top of each artichoke, and it should be rubbed in well to ensure that it adheres.
4. Add the stock to the crockpot with the artichokes.
5. 4 hours of cooking on low settings
6. Warm artichokes are best served.

Ginger Glazed Tofu

Servings: 6
Cooking Time: 2 1/4 Hours
Ingredients:

- 12 oz. firm tofu, cubed
- 1 tablespoon hot sauce
- 1 teaspoon grated ginger
- 2 tablespoons soy sauce
- 1/2 cup vegetable stock

Directions:

1. Soy sauce, ginger, and hot sauce are used to season the tofu. Put the tofu in your slow cooker.
2. Cook for two hours on high after adding the stock.

3. Warm tofu should be served with your preferred side dish.

Cumin Rice

Servings: 6
Cooking Time: 3.5 Hours
Ingredients:
- 2 cups long-grain rice
- 5 cups chicken stock
- 1 teaspoon cumin seeds
- 1 teaspoon olive oil
- 1 tablespoon cream cheese

Directions:
1. In the skillet, heat the olive oil.
2. Adding cumin seeds, toast them for two to three minutes.
3. After that, add the roasted cumin seeds to the crock pot.
4. Rice and chickens are added. Very gently combine the ingredients.
5. Rice should be cooked for 3.5 hours on high with the lid closed.
6. Next, add cream cheese and thoroughly stir the rice.

Nutrition Info: Per Serving: 247 calories, 5.2g protein, 50.1g carbohydrates, 2.3g fat, 0.8g fiber, 2mg cholesterol, 645mg sodium, 91mg potassium.

Sweet Popcorn

Servings: 4
Cooking Time: 20 Minutes

Ingredients:
- 2 cups popped popcorn
- 2 tablespoons butter
- 2 tablespoons brown sugar
- ½ teaspoon ground cinnamon

Directions:
1. Put sugar and butter in the slow cooker.
2. Cook the mixture on high for 15 minutes after adding the ground cinnamon.
3. Then remove the cover, stir the liquid, and add the popcorn that has been popped.
4. Use the spatula to carefully combine the ingredients, then cook on high for an additional 5 minutes.

Nutrition Info: Per Serving: 84 calories, 0.6g protein, 7.8g carbohydrates, 5.9g fat, 0.7g fiber, 15mg cholesterol, 43mg sodium, 22mg potassium.

Butter Pink Rice

Servings: 6
Cooking Time: 5.5 Hours
Ingredients:
- 1 cup pink rice
- 1 cups chicken stock
- 1 teaspoon cream cheese
- 1 tablespoon butter

Directions:

1. Gently stir after adding all the ingredients to the crock pot.
2. Cook the food on low for 5.5 hours with the lid shut.

Nutrition Info: Per Serving: 122 calories, 2.2g protein, 22.3g carbohydrates, 3g fat, 1g fiber, 6mg cholesterol, 143mg sodium, 52mg potassium.

Eggplant Parmigiana

Servings: 6
Cooking Time: 8 1/4 Hours
Ingredients:

- 4 medium eggplants, peeled and finely sliced
- 1/4 cup all-purpose flour
- 4 cups marinara sauce
- 1 cup grated Parmesan
- Salt and pepper to taste

Directions:

1. The eggplants should be salted, peppered, and floured.
2. In the crock pot, arrange the marinara sauce and eggplant slices in layers.
3. Add the shredded cheese on top and simmer for 8 hours on low.
4. Whether warm or cold, serve the parmigiana.

Coffee Beef Roast

Servings: 6
Cooking Time: 4 1/4 Hours

Ingredients:

- 2 pounds beef sirloin
- 2 tablespoons olive oil
- 4 garlic cloves, minced
- 1 cup strong brewed coffee
- 1/2 cup beef stock
- Salt and pepper to taste

Directions:

1. In your crockpot, combine all the ingredients and season with salt and pepper to taste.
2. Cook for four hours on high with a lid on top.
3. Along with your preferred side dish, serve the roast warm and fresh.

Ginger Slow Roasted Pork

Servings: 8
Cooking Time: 7 1/4 Hours
Ingredients:

- 4 pounds pork shoulder
- 2 teaspoons grated ginger
- 1 tablespoon soy sauce
- 1 tablespoon honey
- 1 1/2 cups vegetables stock
- Salt and pepper to taste

Directions:

1. Add honey, soy sauce, ginger, and salt and pepper to the pork for seasoning.
2. Add the stock to your crock pot along with the pork.
3. 7 hours on low heat with a cover over the food.

4. Warm up the pork and serve it with your preferred side dish.

Bacon Millet

Servings: 6
Cooking Time: 6 Hours
Ingredients:
- 2 cups millet
- 4 cups of water
- 2 tablespoons butter
- ½ teaspoon salt
- 2 oz bacon, chopped, cooked

Directions:
1. In the crock pot, add salt and millet.
2. Cook the food on low for six hours after adding water.
3. After cooking the millet, gently combine it with butter and place it on the serving dishes.

Nutrition Info: Per Serving: 337 calories, 10.9g protein, 48.7g carbohydrates, 10.6g fat, 5.7g fiber, 21mg cholesterol, 447mg sodium, 186mg potassium.

Green Enchilada Pork Roast

Servings: 8
Cooking Time: 8 1/4 Hours
Ingredients:
- 4 pounds pork roast
- 2 cups green enchilada sauce
- 1/2 cup chopped cilantro
- 2 chipotle peppers, chopped
- 1/2 cup vegetable stock

- Salt and pepper to taste

Directions:
1. In your Crock Pot, mix the enchilada sauce, cilantro, chipotles, and stock.
2. Salt and pepper the pork roast before adding it.
3. 8 hours of cooking on low settings
4. Warm up the pork and serve it with your preferred side dish.

Mushroom Rissoto

Servings: 4
Cooking Time: 2.5 Hours
Ingredients:
- 1 cup cremini mushrooms, chopped
- 1 tablespoon cream cheese
- 1 cup basmati rice
- cups chicken stock

Directions:
1. In the crock pot, combine basmati rice and chicken stock.
2. Place cremini mushrooms in the dish and cover.
3. For two hours, cook the risotto on high.
4. After that, stir the cream cheese into the rice. More than 30 minutes of cooking on high

Nutrition Info: Per Serving: 186 calories, 4.2g protein, 38.1g carbohydrates, 1.4g fat, 0.7g fiber,

3mg cholesterol, 297mg sodium, 142mg potassium

Mustard Short Ribs

Servings: 2
Cooking Time: 8 Hours
Ingredients:

- 2 beef short ribs, bone in and cut into individual ribs
- Salt and black pepper to the taste
- ½ cup BBQ sauce
- 1 tablespoon mustard
- 1 tablespoon green onions, chopped

Directions:

1. Mix the ribs with the sauce and the remaining ingredients in your
2. Crock Pot; toss, cover, and cook on low for 8 hours.
   Serve the mixture by dividing it among plates.

Nutrition Info: calories 284, fat 7, 4, carbs 18, protein 20

Deviled Chicken

Servings: 4
Cooking Time: 6 1/4 Hours
Ingredients:

- 4 chicken breasts
- 1 cup tomato sauce
- 1/2 cup hot sauce
- 2 tablespoons butter
- 4 garlic cloves, minced
- Salt and pepper to taste

Directions:

1. Put every item into your crock pot.
2. Place a lid on top after adding salt and pepper.
3. Cook for six hours at a low temperature.
4. Warm and fresh chicken should be served.

Vegetable & Vegetarian Recipes

Garlic Gnocchi

Servings: 4
Cooking Time: 3 Hours
Ingredients:

- 2 cups mozzarella, shredded
- 3 egg yolks, beaten
- 1 teaspoon garlic, minced
- ½ cup heavy cream
- Salt and pepper to taste

Directions:

1. Combine the mozzarella and egg yolks in a mixing bowl.
2. Gnocchi should be formed into balls and chilled to set.
3. The gnocchi balls should be dropped into a pot of boiling water and left for 30 seconds. Remove them and add them to the slow cooker.
4. Garlic and heavy cream should be added to the crockpot.
5. To taste, add salt and pepper to the food.
6. Close the lid and cook on low for 3 hours or on high for 1 hour.

Nutrition Info: Calories per serving: 178; Carbohydrates: 4.1g; Protein:20.5 g; Fat: 8.9g; Sugar:0.3g; Sodium: 421mg; Fiber: 2.1g

Garlic Butter

Servings: 8
Cooking Time: 20 Minutes
Ingredients:

- 1 cup vegan butter
- 1 tablespoon garlic powder
- ¼ cup fresh dill, chopped

Directions:

1. Cook everything in the crock pot for 20 minutes on high. When the butter is solid, pour the liquid into the ice cube molds and place them in the refrigerator for 30 minutes.

Nutrition Info: Per Serving: 211 calories, 0.7g protein, 1.6g carbohydrates, 23.1g fat, 0.3g fiber, 61mg cholesterol, 167mg sodium, 68mg potassium.

Cauliflower Rice

Servings: 6
Cooking Time: 2 Hours
Ingredients:

- 4 cups cauliflower, shredded
- 1 cup vegetable stock
- 1 cup of water
- 1 tablespoon cream cheese
- 1 teaspoon dried oregano

Directions:

1. Place each ingredient in the slow cooker.

2. Cauliflower rice should be cooked for two hours on high with the lid closed.

Nutrition Info: Per Serving: 25 calories, 0.8g protein, 3.9g carbohydrates, 0.8g fat, 1.8g fiber, 2mg cholesterol, 153mg sodium, 211mg potassium

Mushroom Steaks

Servings: 4
Cooking Time: 2 Hours
Ingredients

- Portobello mushrooms
- 1 tablespoon avocado oil
- 1 tablespoon lemon juice
- 2 tablespoons coconut cream
- ½ teaspoon ground black pepper

Directions:

1. Sliced Portobello mushrooms are seasoned with coconut cream, lemon juice, avocado oil, and freshly ground black pepper.
2. Afterward, layer the mushroom steaks in the Crock Pot.
3. For one hour, cook the food on high.

Nutrition Info: Per Serving: 43 calories, 3.3g protein, 3.9g carbohydrates, 2.3g fat, 1.4g fiber, 0mg cholesterol, 2mg sodium, 339mg potassium.

Carrot Strips

Servings: 2
Cooking Time: 1 Hour
Ingredients:

- 2 carrots, peeled
- 2 tablespoons sunflower oil
- 1 teaspoon dried thyme
- ½ teaspoon salt
- ½ cup of water

Directions:

1. Carrots should be cut into strips.
2. After that, warm the sunflower oil in the skillet.
3. Roast the carrot strips for two to three minutes on each side in the hot oil.
4. Fill up the crock pot with water.
5. Incorporate salt and dried thyme.
6. After that, add the roasted carrot and cook the meal for an hour on high.

Nutrition Info: Per Serving: 150 calories, 0.6g protein, 6.3g carbohydrates, 14g fat, 1.7g fiber, 0mg cholesterol, 625mg sodium, 200mg potassium.

Ranch Broccoli

Servings: 3
Cooking Time: 1.5 Hours
Ingredients:

- 3 cups broccoli
- 1 teaspoon chili flakes
- 2 tablespoons ranch dressing
- 2 cups of water

Directions:

1. In the slow cooker, place the broccoli.
2. Close the lid after adding water.
3. For 1.5 hours, cook the broccoli on high.
4. After that, drain the broccoli's water and place it in the bowl.
5. Ranch dressing and chili flakes should be added. Gently shake the meal.

Nutrition Info: Per Serving: 34 calories, 2.7g protein, 6.6g carbohydrates, 0.3g fat, 2.4g fiber, 0mg cholesterol, 91mg sodium, 291mg potassium.

Crockpot Baked Tofu

Servings: 4
Cooking Time: 2 Hours
Ingredients:

- 1 small package extra firm tofu, sliced
- 3 tablespoons soy sauce
- 1 tablespoon sesame oil
- 2 teaspoons minced garlic
- Juice from ½ lemon, freshly squeezed

Directions:

1. Combine the soy sauce, sesame oil, garlic, and lemon in a deep dish. If the sauce is too thick, stir in a few tablespoons of water.
2. Slices of tofu should be marinated for at least 2 hours.
3. Cooking spray and foil are used to line and grease the crockpot.
4. Put the marinated tofu slices in the slow cooker.
5. Cook for 4 hours on low or 2 hours on high.
6. Check to see if the tofu slices have a crispy exterior.

Nutrition Info: Calories per serving:145; Carbohydrates: 4.1g; Protein: 11.6g; Fat: 10.8g; Sugar: 0.6g; Sodium: 142mg; Fiber:1.5 g

Sautéed Endives

Servings: 4
Cooking Time: 40 Minutes
Ingredients:

- 1-pound endives, roughly chopped
- ½ cup of water
- 1 tablespoon avocado oil
- 1 teaspoon garlic, diced
- 2 tablespoons coconut cream

Directions:

1. Fill up the crock pot with water.
2. Include garlic and endives.

3. Cook them for 30 minutes on high with the lid closed.
4. Avocado oil and coconut cream are then added.
5. Cook the endives for an additional 10 minutes.

Nutrition Info: Per Serving: 42 calories, 1.9g protein, 4.4g carbohydrates, 2.4g fat, 3.7g fiber, 6mg cholesterol, 41mg sodium, 376mg potassium.

Green Peas Puree

Servings: 2
Cooking Time: 1 Hour
Ingredients:
- 2 cups green peas, frozen
- 1 tablespoon coconut oil
- 1 teaspoon smoked paprika
- 1 cup vegetable stock

Directions:
1. In the crock pot, combine green peas, smoked paprika, and vegetable stock.
2. For an hour, cook the ingredients on high.
3. After that, drain the liquid and use a potato masher to mash the green peas.
4. Stir the cooked puree carefully while adding coconut oil.

Nutrition Info: Per Serving: 184 calories, 8.4g protein, 21.9g carbohydrates, 7.8g fat, 7.8g fiber,

0mg cholesterol, 389mg sodium, 386mg potassium.

Creamy Puree

Servings: 4
Cooking Time: 4 Hours
Ingredients:
- 2 cups potatoes, chopped
- 3 cups of water
- 1 tablespoon vegan butter
- ¼ cup cream
- 1 teaspoon salt

Directions:
1. Fill up the crock pot with water.
2. Add salt and potatoes.
3. For four hours on high, cook the vegetables.
4. Next, add butter and cream after draining the water.
5. Smoothly mash the potatoes.

Nutrition Info: Per Serving: 87 calories, 1.4g protein, 12.3g carbohydrates, 3.8g fat, 1.8g fiber, 10mg cholesterol, 617mg sodium, 314mg potassium

Tomato Okra

Servings: 2
Cooking Time: 6 Hours
Ingredients:
- 2 cups okra, sliced
- 1 teaspoon chili powder
- 1 teaspoon salt
- 1 cup tomato juice

- ¼ cup fresh parsley, chopped

Directions:

1. Carefully combine all the ingredients in the crock pot.
2. Cook the okra on low for 6 hours with the lid shut.

Nutrition Info: Per Serving: 67 calories, 3.2g protein, 13.8g carbohydrates, 0.5g fat, 4.4g fiber, 0mg cholesterol, 1514mg sodium, 644mg potassium.

Garlic Sweet Potato

Servings: 4
Cooking Time: 6 Hours
Ingredients:

- 2-pounds sweet potatoes, chopped
- 1 teaspoon minced garlic
- 2 tablespoons vegan butter
- 1 teaspoon salt
- 3 cups of water

Directions:

1. Fill up the crock pot with water. Swedish should be added.
2. After salting, cover the pot.
3. For six hours, cook the sweet potato on low heat.
4. After that, pour the water off the vegetables and place them in a large bowl.

5. Add butter and minced garlic. Stir the sweet potatoes gently until the butter has melted.

Nutrition Info: Per Serving: 320 calories, 3.6g protein, 63.5g carbohydrates, 6.2g fat, 9.3g fiber, 15mg cholesterol, 648mg sodium, 1857mg potassium.

Mashed Turnips

Servings: 6
Cooking Time: 7 Hours
Ingredients:

- 3-pounds turnip, chopped
- 3 cups of water
- 1 tablespoon vegan butter
- 1 tablespoon chives, chopped
- 2 oz Parmesan, grated

Directions:

1. Place turnips in the slow cooker.
2. Cook the vegetables on low for seven hours while adding water.
3. The turnips should then be drained and mashed.
4. Butter, Parmesan, and chives are added.
5. Melt the butter and Parmesan in the mixture with caution.
6. The chives next. turnips that have been mashed again.

Nutrition Info: Per Serving: 162 calories, 8.6g protein, 15.1g

carbohydrates, 8.1g fat, 4.1g fiber, 22mg cholesterol, 475mg sodium, 490mg potassium.

Chili Dip

Servings: 5
Cooking Time: 5 Hours
Ingredients:

- 5 oz chilies, canned, chopped
- 3 oz Mozzarella, shredded
- 1 tomato, chopped
- ½ cup milk
- 1 teaspoon cornflour

Directions:

1. Blend the milk and corn flour together using a whisk. Fill the crock pot with the liquid.
2. Add the tomato, mozzarella, and chilies after that.
3. Cook the dip on low for five hours with the lid on.

Nutrition Info: Per Serving: 156 calories, 8.7g protein, 22.5g carbohydrates, 5.2g fat, 8.3g fiber, 11mg cholesterol, 140mg sodium, 575mg potassium.

Side Dish Recipes

Mango Rice

Servings: 2
Cooking Time: 2 Hours
Ingredients:
- 1 cup rice
- 2 cups chicken stock
- ½ cup mango, peeled and cubed
- Salt and black pepper to the taste
- 1 teaspoon olive oil

Directions:
1. Mix the rice with the stock and the remaining ingredients in your
2. Crock Pot, toss, cover, and cook on high for two hours.
3. After dividing, serve as a side dish on plates.

Nutrition Info: calories 152, fat 4, fiber 5, carbs 18, protein 4

Rosemary Potatoes

Servings: 12
Cooking Time: 3 Hours
Ingredients:
- 2 tablespoons olive oil
- 3 pounds new potatoes, halved
- 7 garlic cloves, minced
- 1 tablespoon rosemary, chopped
- A pinch of salt and black pepper

Directions:
1. Cook potatoes, garlic, rosemary, salt, and pepper in oil in a crock pot for three hours on high.
2. After dividing, serve as a side dish on plates.

Nutrition Info: calories 102, fat 2, fiber 2, carbs 18, protein 2

Buttery Mushrooms

Servings: 6
Cooking Time: 4 Hours
Ingredients:
- 1 yellow onion, chopped
- 1 pounds mushrooms, halved
- ½ cup butter, melted
- 1 teaspoon Italian seasoning
- Salt and black pepper to the taste
- 1 teaspoon sweet paprika

Directions:
1. Mushrooms should be combined with onions, butter, Italian seasoning, salt, pepper, and paprika in your Crock Pot before being covered and cooked on low for 4 hours.
2. After dividing, serve as a side dish on plates.

Nutrition Info: calories 120, fat 6, fiber 1, carbs 8, protein 4

Beets And Carrots

Servings: 8
Cooking Time: 7 Hours
Ingredients:

- 2 tablespoons stevia
- ¾ cup pomegranate juice
- 2 teaspoons ginger, grated
- 2 and ½ pounds beets, peeled and cut into wedges
- 12 ounces carrots, cut into medium wedges

Directions:

1. Beets, carrots, ginger, stevia, and pomegranate juice should be combined in your Crock Pot and cooked on Low for 7 hours.
2. Place on plates as a side dish after being divided.

Nutrition Info: calories 125, fat 0, fiber 4, carbs 28, protein 3

Maple Sweet Potatoes

Servings: 10
Cooking Time: 5 Hours
Ingredients:

- 8 sweet potatoes, halved and sliced
- 1 cup walnuts, chopped
- ½ cup cherries, dried and chopped
- ½ cup maple syrup
- ¼ cup apple juice

- A pinch of salt

Directions:

1. In your crock pot, arrange the sweet potatoes. Then, add the walnuts, dried cherries, maple syrup, apple juice, and a pinch of salt. toss to combine. Finally, cover and cook on low for 5 hours.
2. After dividing, serve as a side dish on plates.

Nutrition Info: calories 271, fat 6, fiber 4, carbs 26, protein 6

Sage Sweet Potatoes

Servings: 2
Cooking Time: 3 Hours
Ingredients:

- ½ pound sweet potatoes, thinly sliced
- 1 tablespoon sage, chopped
- 2 tablespoons orange juice
- A pinch of salt and black pepper
- ½ cup veggie stock
- ½ tablespoon olive oil

Directions:

1. Mix the potatoes with the sage and the other ingredients in your
2. Crock Pot; toss, cover, and cook on high for three hours.
3. After dividing, serve as a side dish on plates.

Nutrition Info: calories 189, fat 4, fiber 4, carbs 17, protein 4

Beans And Red Peppers

Servings: 2
Cooking Time: 2 Hrs.
Ingredients:
- 2 cups green beans, halved
- 1 red bell pepper, cut into strips
- Salt and black pepper to the taste
- 1 tbsp olive oil
- 1 and ½ tbsp honey mustard

Directions:
1. To the crock pot, add green beans, honey mustard, red bell pepper, oil, salt, and black pepper.
2. Put the lid on the cooker and select the high cooking setting for 2 hours.
3. Serve hot.

Nutrition Info: Per Serving: Calories: 50, Total Fat: 0g, Fiber: 4g, Total Carbs: 8g, Protein: 2g

Pink Rice

Servings: 8
Cooking Time: 5 Hours
Ingredients:
- 1 teaspoon salt
- 2 and ½ cups water
- 2 cups pink rice

Directions:

1. Rice should be added to your Crock Pot along with water, salt, and a cover to cook on low for five hours.
2. Serve rice as a side dish by giving it a little stir and dividing it among plates.

Nutrition Info: calories 120, fat 3, fiber 3, carbs 16, protein 4

Green Beans And Red Peppers

Servings: 2
Cooking Time: 2 Hours
Ingredients:
- 2 cups green beans, halved
- 1 red bell pepper, cut into strips
- Salt and black pepper to the taste
- 1 tablespoon olive oil
- 1 and ½ tablespoon honey mustard

Directions:
1. Green beans should be combined with bell pepper, oil, honey mustard, salt, and pepper in your Crock Pot before being covered and cooked on high for two hours.
2. After dividing, serve as a side dish on plates.

Nutrition Info: calories 50, fat 0, fiber 4, carbs 8, protein 2

Cumin Quinoa Pilaf

Servings: 2
Cooking Time: 2 Hours
Ingredients:
- 1 cup quinoa
- 2 teaspoons butter, melted
- Salt and black pepper to the taste
- 1 teaspoon turmeric powder
- 2 cups chicken stock
- 1 teaspoon cumin, ground

Directions:
1. To prepare, butter your Crock Pot, add the quinoa and the remaining ingredients, toss, cover, and cook on high for two hours.
2. After dividing, serve as a side dish on plates.

Nutrition Info: calories 152, fat 3, fiber 6, carbs 8, protein 4

Chicken With Sweet Potato

Servings: 6
Cooking Time: 3 Hours
Ingredients:
- 16 oz. sweet potato, peeled and diced
- 3 cups chicken stock
- 1 tbsp salt
- 3 tbsp margarine
- 2 tbsp cream cheese

Directions:
1. Salt, chicken stock, and sweet potatoes should be added to the crock pot.
2. Place the lid on the cooker and select a cooking time of 5 hours on high.
3. Potatoes that have been cooked slowly should be drained and placed in a bowl.
4. Sweet potatoes are mashed with cream cheese and margarine added.
5. Present fresh.

Nutrition Info: Per Serving: Calories: 472, Total Fat: 31.9g, Fiber: 6.7g, Total Carbs: 43.55g, Protein: 3g

Mexican Avocado Rice

Servings: 8
Cooking Time: 4 Hrs
Ingredients:
- 1 cup long-grain rice
- 1 and ¼ cups veggie stock
- ½ cup cilantro, chopped
- ½ avocado, pitted, peeled and chopped
- Salt and black pepper to the taste
- ¼ cup green hot sauce

Directions:
1. Fill the crock pot with stock and rice.
2. Put the lid on the cooker and select the low setting for 4 hours of cooking time.

3. In the meantime, mix avocado flesh with hot sauce, cilantro, salt, and black pepper.
4. With the avocado sauce on top, serve the cooked rice.

Nutrition Info: Per Serving: Calories: 100, Total Fat: 3g, Fiber: 6g, Total Carbs: 18g, Protein: 4g

Italian Eggplant

Servings: 2
Cooking Time: 2 Hours
Ingredients:
- 2 small eggplants, roughly cubed
- ½ cup heavy cream
- Salt and black pepper to the taste
- 1 tablespoon olive oil
- A pinch of hot pepper flakes
- 2 tablespoons oregano, chopped

Directions:
1. Mix the eggplants with the cream and the remaining ingredients in your Crock Pot; toss, cover, and cook on high for two hours.
2. After dividing, serve as a side dish on plates.

Nutrition Info: calories 132, fat 4, fiber 6, carbs 12, protein 3

Garlicky Black Beans

Servings: 8

Cooking Time: 7 Hours
Ingredients:
- 1 cup black beans, soaked overnight, drained and rinsed
- 1 cup of water
- Salt and black pepper to the taste
- 1 spring onion, chopped
- 2 garlic cloves, minced
- ½ tsp cumin seeds

Directions:
1. To the crock pot, add the beans, salt, black pepper, cumin seeds, garlic, and onion.
2. Put the lid on the cooker and select the low setting for 7 hours of cooking time.
3. Serve hot.

Nutrition Info: Per Serving: Calories: 300, Total Fat: 4g, Fiber: 6g, Total Carbs: 20g, Protein: 15g

Lemon Artichokes

Servings: 2
Cooking Time: 3 Hours
Ingredients:
- 1 cup veggie stock
- 2 medium artichokes, trimmed
- 1 tablespoon lemon juice
- 1 tablespoon lemon zest, grated
- Salt to the taste

Directions:

1. Mix the artichokes with the stock and the other ingredients in your Crock Pot, toss, cover, and cook on low for three hours.
2. Artichokes should be divided between plates and served as a side dish.

Nutrition Info: calories 100, fat 2, fiber 5, carbs 10, protein 4

Mexican Rice

Servings: 8
Cooking Time: 4 Hours
Ingredients:
- 1 cup long grain rice
- 1 and ¼ cups veggie stock
- ½ cup cilantro, chopped
- ½ avocado, pitted, peeled and chopped
- Salt and black pepper to the taste
- ¼ cup green hot sauce

Directions:
1. Rice should be added to your Crock Pot, along with stock, and cooked on low for 4 hours before being fluffed with a fork and transferred to a bowl.
2. Avocado, hot sauce, and cilantro should all be combined in a food processor and blended well before being poured over rice, mixed well,

and served as a side dish after adding salt and pepper.

Nutrition Info: calories 100, fat 3, fiber 6, carbs 18, protein 4

Rosemary Leeks

Servings: 2
Cooking Time: 3 Hours
Ingredients:
- ½ tablespoon olive oil
- ½ leeks, sliced
- ½ cup tomato sauce
- 2 garlic cloves, minced
- Salt and black pepper to the taste
- ¼ tablespoon rosemary, chopped

Directions:
1. Mix the leeks with the oil, sauce, and other ingredients in your
2. Crock Pot, toss, cover, and cook on high for 3 hours. Then, divide the mixture between plates and serve as a side dish.

Nutrition Info: calories 202, fat 2, fiber 6, carbs 18, protein 8

Okra Mix

Servings: 4
Cooking Time: 8 Hours
Ingredients:
- 2 garlic cloves, minced
- 1 yellow onion, chopped
- 14 ounces tomato sauce

- 1 teaspoon sweet paprika
- 2 cups okra, sliced
- Salt and black pepper to the taste

Directions:

1. Combine the garlic, onion, tomato sauce, paprika, okra, salt, and pepper in your Crock Pot. Cover and cook on low for 8 hours.
2. After dividing, serve as a side dish on plates.

Nutrition Info: calories 200, fat 6, fiber 5, carbs 10, protein 4

Roasted Beets

Servings: 5
Cooking Time: 4 Hours
Ingredients:

- 10 small beets
- 5 teaspoons olive oil
- A pinch of salt and black pepper

Directions:

1. Each beet should be placed on a sheet of tin foil. Drizzle with oil, sprinkle with salt and pepper, and rub in well. Wrap the beets in the foil, put them in your Crock Pot, cover it, and cook on high for 4 hours.
2. Beets should be opened, allowed to cool slightly, then peeled, sliced, and served as a side dish.

Nutrition Info: calories 100, fat 2, fiber 2, carbs 4, protein 5

Orange Carrots Mix

Servings: 2
Cooking Time: 6 Hours
Ingredients:

- ½ pound carrots, sliced
- A pinch of salt and black pepper
- ½ tablespoon olive oil
- ½ cup orange juice
- ½ teaspoon orange rind, grated

Directions:

1. Mix the carrots with the oil and the remaining ingredients in your
2. Crock Pot, toss, cover, and cook on low for 6 hours.
3. After dividing, serve as a side dish on plates.

Nutrition Info: calories 140, fat 2, fiber 2, carbs 7, protein 6

Dill Cauliflower Mash

Servings: 6
Cooking Time: 5 Hours
Ingredients:

- 1 cauliflower head, florets separated
- 1/3 cup dill, chopped
- 6 garlic cloves
- 2 tablespoons butter, melted

- A pinch of salt and black pepper

Directions:

1. Put the cauliflower in the crock pot, cover it with water, and cook on high for 5 hours. Add the dill, garlic, and water.

2. Drain the cauliflower and dill, then combine with the butter, salt, and pepper. Using a potato masher, mash the mixture until smooth.

Nutrition Info: calories 187, fat 4, fiber 5, carbs 12, protein 3

Snack Recipes

Apple Dip

Servings: 8
Cooking Time: 1 Hour And 30 Minutes
Ingredients:
- 5 apples, peeled and chopped
- ½ teaspoon cinnamon powder
- 12 ounces jarred caramel sauce
- A pinch of nutmeg, ground

Directions:
1. Cook the apples in your Crock Pot for 1 hour and 30 minutes on high after combining them with the cinnamon, caramel sauce, and nutmeg.
2. Serve in bowls after dividing.

Nutrition Info: calories 200, fat 3, fiber 6, carbs 10, protein 5

Apple Sausage Snack

Servings: 15
Cooking Time: 2 Hrs
Ingredients:
- 2 lbs. sausages, sliced
- 18 oz. apple jelly
- 9 oz. Dijon mustard

Directions:
1. To the slow cooker, add apple jelly, mustard, and sausage slices.

2. Put the lid on the cooker and select the low setting for 2 hours of cooking time.
3. Present fresh.

Nutrition Info: Per Serving: Calories: 200, Total Fat: 3g, Fiber: 1g, Total Carbs: 9g, Protein: 10g

Spinach Dip

Servings: 2
Cooking Time: 1 Hour
Ingredients:
- 2 tablespoons heavy cream
- ½ cup Greek yogurt
- ½ pound baby spinach
- 2 garlic cloves, minced
- Salt and black pepper to the taste

Directions:
1. Mix the spinach with the cream and the other ingredients in your
2. Crock Pot; toss, cover, and cook on high for an hour.
3. Use as a party dip by blending with an immersion blender, dividing into bowls, and serving.

Nutrition Info: calories 221, fat 5, fiber 7, carbs 12, protein 5

Spicy Dip

Servings: 10

Cooking Time: 3 Hours
Ingredients:
- 1 pound spicy sausage, chopped
- 8 ounces cream cheese, soft
- 8 ounces sour cream
- 20 ounces canned tomatoes and green chilies, chopped

Directions:
1. Combine sausage with cream cheese, sour cream, tomatoes, and chilies in your Crock Pot. Stir, cover, and cook on low for three hours.
2. Serve as a snack after being divided into bowls.

Nutrition Info: calories 300, fat 12, fiber 7, carbs 30, protein 34

Corn Dip

Servings: 2
Cooking Time: 2 Hours
Ingredients:
- 1 cup corn
- 1 tablespoon chives, chopped
- ½ cup heavy cream
- 2 ounces cream cheese, cubed
- ¼ teaspoon chili powder

Directions:
1. Mix the corn with the chives and the other ingredients in your

2. Crock Pot; stir to combine; then cover and cook on low for two hours.
3. After dividing, dish up and serve as a dip.

Nutrition Info: calories 272, fat 5, fiber 10, carbs 12, protein 4

Apple Jelly Sausage Snack

Servings: 15
Cooking Time: 2 Hours
Ingredients:
- 2 pounds sausages, sliced
- 18 ounces apple jelly
- 9 ounces Dijon mustard

Directions:
1. In your crock pot, add the sausage slices, apple jelly, and mustard.
2. Toss to combine, then cover and cook on low for two hours.
3. Serve as a snack after being divided into bowls.

Nutrition Info: calories 200, fat 3, fiber 1, carbs 9, protein 10

Roasted Parmesan Green Beans

Servings: 8 (4.4 Ounces Per Serving)
Cooking Time: 4 Hours And 5 Minutes
Ingredients:
- 2 lbs. green beans, fresh, trimmed
- 2 tablespoons olive oil

- 1 teaspoon salt and black pepper
- ½ cup Parmesan cheese, grated

Directions:

1. Green beans should be rinsed and dried with paper towels. Add salt and pepper and drizzle with olive oil. Spread out the beans without touching one another after evenly coating them in olive oil with your fingers.
2. Green beans should be placed in a greased Crock-Pot. Add some Parmesan cheese.
3. Cook covered for 3-4 hours on HIGH. Serve.

Nutrition Info: Calories: 91.93, Total Fat: 5.41 g, Saturated Fat: 1.6 g, Cholesterol: 5.5 mg, Sodium: 337.43 mg, Potassium: 247.12 mg, Total Carbohydrates: 6.16 g, Fiber: 3.06 g, Sugar: 3.75 g, Protein: 4.48 g

Lemony Artichokes

Servings: 4 (5.2 Ounces Per Serving)
Cooking Time: 4 Hours And 10 Minutes

Ingredients:

- 4 artichokes
- 2 tablespoons coconut butter, melted

- 3 tablespoons lemon juice
- 1 teaspoon sea salt
- Ground black pepper to taste

Directions:

1. Get the artichokes clean. Till you reach the paler yellow leaves, pull off the outermost leaves. Trim the artichokes' top third or so.
2. Trim the stems' bottoms. Put it in a crock pot. Pour over the artichokes after combining the melted coconut butter, salt, and lemon juice.
3. Cook covered for 6 to 8 hours on low or 3 to 4 hours on high. Serve.

Nutrition Info: Calories: 113.58, Total Fat: 5.98 g, Saturated Fat: 3.7 g, Cholesterol: 15.27 mg, Sodium: 702.59 mg, Potassium: 487.2 mg, Total Carbohydrates: 8.25 g, Fiber: 6.95 g, Sugar: 1.56 g, Protein: 4.29 g

Onion Dip

Servings: 6
Cooking Time: 1 Hour

Ingredients:

- 8 ounces cream cheese, soft
- ¾ cup sour cream
- 1 cup cheddar cheese, shredded

- 10 bacon slices, cooked and chopped
- 2 yellow onions, chopped

Directions:

1. Mix the cream cheese, sour cream, cheddar cheese, bacon, and onion in your Crock Pot. Cover and cook on High for an hour.
2. Serve in bowls after dividing.

Nutrition Info: calories 222, fat 4, fiber 6, carbs 17, protein 4

Salsa Beans Dip

Servings: 2
Cooking Time: 1 Hour
Ingredients:

- ¼ cup salsa
- 1 cup canned red kidney beans, drained and rinsed
- ½ cup mozzarella, shredded
- 1 tablespoon green onions, chopped

Directions:

1. Mix the salsa with the beans and the other ingredients in your
2. Crock Pot, toss, and then cook on high for an hour.
3. Serve as a party dip after being divided into bowls.

Nutrition Info: calories 302, fat 5, fiber 10, carbs 16, protein 6

Almond Buns

Servings: 6 (1.9 Ounces Per Serving)
Cooking Time: 20 Minutes
Ingredients:

- 3 cups almond flour
- 5 tablespoons butter
- 1 ½ teaspoons sweetener of your choice (optional)
- 2 eggs
- 1 ½ teaspoons baking powder

Directions:

1. The dry ingredients should be combined in a mixing bowl. Whisk the eggs in another bowl. Mix well after adding the melted butter.
2. Equally divide the almond mixture into six portions. Place six almond buns in the crock-pot after greasing the bottom. With the cover on, cook on HIGH for 2 to 2 1/2 hours or LOW for 4 to 4 1/2 hours. Serve warm.

Nutrition Info: Calories: 219.35, Total Fat: 20.7 g, Saturated Fat: 7.32 g, Cholesterol: 87.44 mg, Sodium: 150.31 mg, Potassium: 145.55 mg, Total Carbohydrates: 4.59 g, Fiber: 1.8 g, Sugar: 1.6 g, Protein: 6.09 g

Bourbon Sausage Bites

Servings: 12

Cooking Time: 3 Hours And 5 Minutes

Ingredients:

- 1/3 cup bourbon
- 1 pound smoked sausage, sliced
- 12 ounces chili sauce
- ¼ cup brown sugar
- 2 tablespoons yellow onion, grated

Directions:

1. Sausage slices are added to a hot pan over medium-high heat, browned for 2 minutes on each side, drained on paper towels, and then placed in your Crock Pot.
2. Cook for 3 hours on low after adding the chili sauce, sugar, onion, and bourbon.
3. Serve as a snack after being divided into bowls.

Nutrition Info: calories 190, fat 11, fiber 1, carbs 12, protein 5

Dessert Recipes

Nutty Caramel Apples

Servings: 6
Cooking Time: 4 Hrs.
Ingredients:
- 6 gala apples, cut in half and deseeded
- 8 oz caramel, package
- 5 tbsp water
- 3 tbsp walnuts, crushed

Directions:
1. Place the apples in a Crock Pot insert along with the water, caramel, and walnuts.
2. Put the lid on the cooker and select the low setting for 3 hours of cooking time.
3. When chilled, serve.

Nutrition Info: Per Serving: Calories: 307, Total Fat: 12g, Fiber: 5g, Total Carbs: 47.17g, Protein: 4g

Chocolate and Liquor Cream

Servings: 4
Cooking Time: 2 Hours
Ingredients:
- 3.5 ounces crème fraiche
- 3.5 ounces dark chocolate, cut into chunks
- 1 teaspoon liquor
- 1 teaspoon sugar

Directions:
1. Creme fraiche, chocolate, alcohol, and sugar should be combined in your Crock Pot and cooked on low for two hours before being divided into bowls and served cold.

Nutrition Info: calories 200, fat 12, fiber 4, carbs 6, protein 3

Espresso Mousse Drink

Servings: 1
Cooking Time: 1 Hour
Ingredients:
- ½ cup milk
- 1 teaspoon instant coffee
- ¼ cup of water

Directions:
1. Water and instant coffee blended
2. After that, add milk to the crock pot and cook it for an hour on high.
3. Use a hand blender to blend the coffee mixture in the background until foamy.
4. Place the glass with the blended mixture inside. put hot milk in.

Nutrition Info: Per Serving: 61 calories, 4g protein, 6g carbohydrates, 2.5g fat, 0g fiber, 10mg cholesterol, 59mg sodium, 73mg potassium.

Cinnamon Peach Mix

Servings: 2
Cooking Time: 2 Hours
Ingredients:

- 2 cups peaches, peeled and halved
- 3 tablespoons sugar
- ½ teaspoon cinnamon powder
- ½ cup heavy cream
- 1 teaspoon vanilla extract

Directions:

1. Mix the peaches with the sugar and the other ingredients in your
2. Crock Pot; stir, cover, and cook on high for two hours.
3. To serve, divide the mixture among bowls.

Nutrition Info: calories 212, fat 4, fiber 4, carbs 7, protein 3

Apple Granola Crumble

Servings: 4
Cooking Time: 6 1/4 Hours
Ingredients:

- 4 red apples, peeled, cored and sliced
- 2 tablespoons honey
- 1 1/2 cups granola
- 1/2 teaspoon cinnamon powder

Directions:

1. In the crock pot, combine the apples and honey.
2. Add cinnamon, and then top with granola.
3. Cook the food for six hours on low heat with the lid on.
4. Warm crumble should be served.

Mandarin Cream

Servings: 2
Cooking Time: 2 Hours
Ingredients:

- 1 tablespoon ginger, grated
- 3 tablespoons sugar
- 3 mandarins, peeled and chopped
- 2 tablespoons agave nectar
- ½ cup coconut cream

Directions:

1. Mix the ginger with the sugar, mandarins, and other ingredients in your crock pot. Whisk everything well. Cover and simmer on high for two hours.
2. Using an immersion blender, puree the cream, then divide it among dishes and serve chilled.

Nutrition Info: calories 100, fat 4, fiber 5, carbs 6, protein 7

Sweet Baked Milk

Servings: 5
Cooking Time: 10 Hours
Ingredients:

- 4 cups of milk
- 3 tablespoons sugar
- ½ teaspoon vanilla extract

Directions:

1. Until the sugar is dissolved, combine the milk, sugar, and vanilla extract.
2. After that, add the liquid to the crock pot and cover it.
   On low, brew the milk for ten hours.

Nutrition Info: Per Serving: 126 calories, 6.4g protein, 16.9g carbohydrates, 4g fat, 3g fiber, 16mg cholesterol, 92mg sodium, 113mg potassium.

Berry Cream

Servings: 2
Cooking Time: 2 Hours
Ingredients:

- 2 tablespoons cashews, chopped
- 1 cup heavy cream
- ½ cup blueberries
- ½ cup maple syrup
- ½ tablespoon coconut oil, melted

Directions:

1. Mix the cream, berries, and other ingredients in your Crock
2. Pot; whisk; cover; and cook on low for 2 hours.
3. Serve the mixture cold and divide it among bowls.

Nutrition Info: calories 200, fat 3, fiber 5, carbs 12, protein 3

Caramel Apple Tart

Servings: 4
Cooking Time: 3.5 Hours
Ingredients:

- 2 tablespoons salted caramel
- 2 apples, sliced
- 1 teaspoon butter
- 5 oz puff pastry
- 1 teaspoon olive oil

Directions:

1. Sprinkle some olive oil inside the Crock Pot bowl.
2. The puff pastry should then be placed inside and shaped like a pie crust.
3. Sliced apples should be placed on top of the butter-greased pie crust.
4. After that, sprinkle salted caramel over the apples and secure the lid.
5. For 3.5 hours on high, bake the apple tart.

Nutrition Info: Per Serving: 291 calories, 3.1g protein, 35.3g carbohydrates, 16.2g fat, 3.2g fiber, 3mg cholesterol, 108mg sodium, 152mg potassium.

Vegan Mousse

Servings: 3

Cooking Time: 2 Hours

Ingredients:

- 1 cup of coconut milk
- 2 tablespoons corn starch
- 1 teaspoon vanilla extract
- 1 avocado, pitted, pilled

Directions:

1. Pour the smooth mixture of coconut milk and corn starch into the slow cooker.
2. Cook it on high for two hours after adding vanilla extract.
3. Then, after the mixture has reached room temperature, add the avocado.
4. The mousse should be smooth and fluffy after blending.

Nutrition Info: Per Serving: 348 calories, 3.1g protein, 16.4g carbohydrates, 32.1g fat, 6.3g fiber, 0mg cholesterol, 16mg sodium, 537mg potassium.

Quinoa Pudding

Servings: 2

Cooking Time: 2 Hours

Ingredients:

- 1 cup quinoa
- 2 cups almond milk
- ½ cup sugar
- ½ tablespoon walnuts, chopped
- ½ tablespoon almonds, chopped

Directions:

1. Mix the quinoa with the milk and the remaining ingredients in your Crock Pot, toss, cover, and cook on high for two hours.
2. Serve the pudding in cups after it has been divided.

Nutrition Info: calories 213, fat 4, fiber 6, carbs 10, protein 4

Easy Monkey Rolls

Servings: 8

Cooking Time: 3 Hours

Ingredients:

- 1 tablespoon liquid honey
- 1 tablespoon sugar
- 2 eggs, beaten
- 1-pound cinnamon rolls, dough
- 2 tablespoons butter, melted

Directions:

1. Cut the dough for the cinnamon rolls into 8 pieces.
2. The rolls are then placed inside the crock pot after it has been lined with baking paper.
3. Combine sugar, egg, butter, and liquid honey in a bowl. The mixture is beaten.
4. Spread out the egg mixture evenly over the dough for the cinnamon rolls.
5. Cook the food for 3 hours on high with the lid closed.

Nutrition Info: Per Serving: 266 calories, 4.9g protein, 32.6g

carbohydrates, 13.3g fat, 1.4g fiber, 86mg cholesterol, 253mg sodium, 80mg potassium.

Tapioca Pearls Pudding

Servings: 6
Cooking Time: 1 Hr.
Ingredients:
- 1 and ¼ cups of milk
- 1/3 cup tapioca pearls, rinsed
- ½ cup of water
- ½ cup of sugar
- Zest of ½ lemon

Directions:
1. In the Crock Pot insert, whisk the tapioca with the milk, sugar, lemon zest, and water.
2. Put the lid on the cooker and select the low setting for 1 hour of cooking time.
3. Serve.

Nutrition Info: Per Serving: Calories: 200, Total Fat: 4g, Fiber: 2g, Total Carbs: 37g, Protein: 3g

Pear Apple Jam

Servings: 12
Cooking Time: 3 Hrs.
Ingredients:
- 8 pears, cored and cut into quarters
- 2 apples, peeled, cored and quartered
- ½ cup apple juice
- 1 tsp cinnamon, ground

Directions:
1. Put cinnamon, apples, pears, and apple juice in the Crock Pot insert.
2. Put the lid on the cooker and select the high setting for 3 hours of cooking time.
3. To make jam, puree this cooked pear-apple mixture.
4. Divide them among the jars and let them cool.
5. Serve.

Nutrition Info: Per Serving: Calories: 100, Total Fat: 1g, Fiber: 2g, Total Carbs: 20g, Protein: 3g

Conclusion

Congratulations! You've reached the end of **"The Ultimate Crock Pot Cookbook for Beginners."** You've embarked on a journey into the world of slow cooking, discovering its myriad benefits, and unlocking the potential of your trusty crock pot. As you close this book, I hope you feel empowered and inspired to continue experimenting with new recipes, flavors, and techniques.

Throughout this cookbook, we've delved into the fundamentals of slow cooking, from understanding the basics of your crock pot to mastering essential techniques for successful meals. We've explored a diverse range of recipes, spanning breakfast, lunch, dinner, and even delectable desserts, all designed with beginners in mind.

But beyond just providing recipes, this book aimed to instill confidence in your culinary abilities. Whether you're a novice in the kitchen or a seasoned cook looking to simplify meal prep, slow cooking offers a convenient and fuss-free solution. By allowing ingredients to simmer and meld together over hours of gentle heat, you can achieve complex flavors and tender textures with minimal effort.

One of the most significant advantages of slow cooking is its versatility. From hearty stews and comforting soups to tender roasts and flavorful curries, the possibilities are endless. With a bit of creativity, you can adapt recipes to suit your preferences, dietary restrictions, or whatever ingredients you have on hand. Don't be afraid to experiment and make each dish your own.

Moreover, slow cooking isn't just about convenience; it's also about nourishment. By using fresh, wholesome ingredients and minimizing the need for added fats or preservatives, you can create meals that are not only delicious but also nutritious. With a focus on whole foods and balanced flavors, you can feel good about what you're putting on the table for yourself and your loved ones.

vered, slow cooking is not about rushing through the
her embracing the journey. It's about savoring the
romas fill your home, eagerly awaiting the moment when
nally dig into a piping hot, soul-satisfying meal. In our fast-
ed world, where time is a precious commodity, slow cooking
encourages us to slow down, take a breath, and enjoy the simple
pleasures of food and fellowship.

I encourage you to continue honing your skills as a slow cook aficionado.
Experiment with different ingredients, spices, and cooking times to
discover what works best for you. Don't be discouraged by the occasional
mishap; even the most experienced cooks encounter setbacks now and
then. Instead, view each challenge as an opportunity to learn and grow in
your culinary journey.

In addition to expanding your repertoire of slow cooker recipes, consider
exploring other aspects of the culinary world. Whether it's mastering the
art of homemade bread, perfecting your knife skills, or learning to pair
wines with your meals, there's always something new to discover in the
realm of food and cooking.

Above all, remember that cooking is not just a chore but a joyful
expression of creativity and care. Whether you're cooking for yourself,
your family, or friends, the act of preparing a meal is an opportunity to
nourish both body and soul. So, embrace the process, savor the flavors,
and cherish the memories created around the table.

As you bid farewell to this cookbook, I hope it serves as a trusted
companion on your culinary adventures for years to come. May your
crock pot continue to be a source of warmth, comfort, and delicious
meals, bringing joy to your kitchen and delight to your taste buds. Happy
slow cooking!

Bon appétit!

Made in the USA
Monee, IL
13 November 2024

70020213R10066